EAST BANK /
WEST BANK

EAST BANK / WEST BANK

Jordan and the Prospects for Peace

ARTHUR R. DAY

Council on Foreign Relations

COUNCIL ON FOREIGN RELATIONS BOOKS

The Council on Foreign Relations, Inc., is a nonprofit and nonpartisan organization devoted to promoting improved understanding of international affairs through the free exchange of ideas. The Council does not take any position on questions of foreign policy and has no affiliation with, and receives no funding from, the United States government.

From time to time, books and monographs written by members of the Council's research staff or visiting fellows, or commissioned by the Council, or written by an independent author with critical review contributed by a Council study or working group are published with the designation "Council on Foreign Relations Book." Any book or monograph bearing that designation is, in the judgment of the Committee on Studies of the Council's board of directors, a responsible treatment of a significant international topic worthy of presentation to the public. All statements of fact and expressions of opinion contained in Council books are, however, the sole responsibility of the author.

Library of Congress Cataloging-in-Publication Data

Day, Arthur R.
    East Bank/West Bank.

    Bibliography: p.
    Includes index.
    1. Jordan—Politics and government.   2. Palestinian Arabs—
Jordan—Politics and government.   3. Jordan—Relations—
United States.   4. United States—Relations—Jordan.   I. Title.
DS154.55.D39   1986   303.4'825695'073   86-8820
ISBN 0-87609-017-X
ISBN 0-87609-016-1 (pbk.)

Contents

Maps

Dedicated to my wife Carol and sons Frank, Peter and Thomas, who shared the trials and satisfactions of Foreign Service life, and helped and encouraged me in writing this book.

Preface

A Council on Foreign Relations study project set out in 1984–1985 to examine the internal political, social and economic dynamics of Jordan today and the ways in which they influence the role the Kingdom plays in the region. This book has developed out of that study.

The Council project was built around a study group of 35 members that met five times from December 1984 through April 1985 to discuss major aspects of Jordanian life. Chaired by Dr. Olin C. Robison , President of Middlebury College, the group represented a wide range of backgrounds, the common denominator being an interest in the Middle East.

In three of these meetings the discussion was opened by Jordanians prominent in the political life of their country who traveled to the United States for the purpose. A leading Jordanian journalist and two American economic experts provided the opening statements for the group's other two meetings. There was no attempt on the part of the study group to draw conclusions or to reach a consensus on the issues discussed. The purpose was rather to gain as clear a picture as possible of the situation in Jordan and the Middle East generally and to subject it to a probing analysis in free-wheeling debate among the members. The Council's custom of protecting the confidentiality of views expressed by group members and visitors encouraged frank debate.

This book owes much to the study group discussions but it is not in any sense a summation of them nor does it purport to represent the views of group members, which may differ from one another and from those set forth in the book. The author was director of the project and participated in all the meetings, profiting greatly from them. Many group members as well as others reviewed early drafts and met with the author to provide detailed and immensely helpful advice and assistance. The resulting book, however, is the sole responsibility of the author. He conducted independent research for it and traveled twice to Jordan—on one such visit going on to Jerusalem and the West Bank— to gather up-to-date impressions and information.

The Council staff was extremely helpful in all stages of the project and of the book itself. Paul Kreisberg, Director of Studies, provided invaluable support with his clear concept of the project's goals, a keen editorial sense and constant encouragement. Janice Murray, Assistant Director of Studies, was a vital and understanding link to the facilities and logistics of the Council. LaVerne Owens, with unfailing cheerfulness, kept a firm hand on the study group and its meetings. David Kellogg, Publications Director, was helpful with advice at every stage of the book's preparation, and he and Editor Robert Valkenier expertly transformed the draft into the text of a book. Susanne Roach and Alice McLoughlin at the word processors successfully coped with successive drafts.

The study group rapporteur, Daniel Darst, deserves special mention for remarkably prompt and accurate reporting of the meetings as well as for some of the detailed research. The project, including the study group, the author's research trips to Jordan, and travel by some of the Jordanian participants, was supported by a grant from the Ford Foundation.

Most importantly, the Council and the author are grateful to the study group members, a list of whom concludes this preface. Dr. Robison was an adept chairman; Professor J.C. Hurewitz of Columbia University generously stepped in to take his place for two meetings. In addition, Paul Jabber, a senior fellow at the Council, Fouad Ajami, John Campbell, Ian Lustick and Mary Wilson, though not members of the group, read drafts and made extensive and invaluable comments.

Members of the Study Group were:

Olin C. Robison,
  Chairman
David Aaron
Col. David Cooper
Larry L. Fabian
Col. Scott Fisher
Peter Grose
George Gruen
Peter Gubser
Najeeb Halaby
Rita E. Hauser
Fred Haynes
Karen Elliott House

J.C. Hurewitz
Charles Issawi
Amos A. Jordan
Paul A. Jureidini
Judith Kipper
William Kirby
Paul Kreisberg
James F. Leonard
Winston Lord
David Lowenfeld
Frank E. Loy
Aaron D. Miller

John O'Connell
Margaret
  Osmer-McQuade
Robert Pelletreau
Don Peretz
James Piscatori
Col. Al Prados
Delwyn Roy
Barry Rubin
Harold H. Saunders
Richard Viets
R. Bayly Winder

Arthur R. Day

New York
February 1986

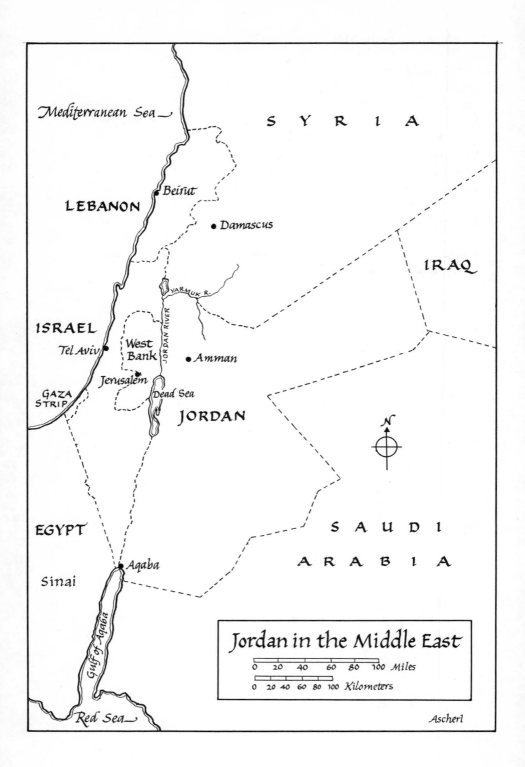

Mediterranean Sea

SYRIA

LEBANON

Beirut

Damascus

IRAQ

YARMUK R.

ISRAEL

Tel Aviv

West Bank

JORDAN RIVER

Amman

Jerusalem

Dead Sea

GAZA STRIP

JORDAN

N

EGYPT

SAUDI

ARABIA

Sinai

Aqaba

Gulf of Aqaba

Red Sea

Jordan in the Middle East

0   20   40   60   80   100 Miles

0   20 40 60 80 100 Kilometers

Ascherl

Introduction

I n the summer of 1985, at a reception given by an Arab mission to the
United Nations, an American journalist encountered an acquaintance just back from a trip to Jordan. The conversation turned to the
future of the country. "If King Hussein and Prince Hassan [next in line
for the throne] should disappear tomorrow," the journalist asked,
"would the Palestinian majority in the country take over?" Those lis-
tening to the conversation offered various responses, but everyone
understood what the journalist was asking: Is Jordan not already a
Palestinian state with a lame duck king, left over from another era?

At about the same time, polls in Israel showed that driving the
Palestinian Arabs out of Israel and the Arab territories occupied by
Israel, presumably into Jordan, was gaining support as a solution to
Israel's Palestinian problem. The principal advocate of this most radical solution, the American Rabbi Meir Kahane, a few years ago considered to be on the lunatic fringe, drew support especially among the
young: 42 percent of high school students in one poll. Ariel Sharon,
bruised after the failure of his Lebanon invasion but still a powerhouse
in the Likud bloc of right-wing parties and a minister in Israeli governments, including the coalition formed in 1984 by Shimon Peres, had
been saying for years that "Jordan is Palestine."

These are extremist voices in the Israeli body politic, but the growing trend toward violent solutions in the Middle East gives some credibility to radical scenarios. The possibility of substantial change in Jordan was suggested, moreover, by the noted Middle East expert, Fouad
Ajami, in a scholarly discussion that is harder to ignore. "Jordan," this

1

expert said, in a New York seminar in the spring of 1985, "is the only player in the Arab-Israeli dispute that has much room left—much plasticity—to absorb change. That's where the changes involved in settling the Palestinian problem will have to come."

These vignettes raise some serious issues. The most simplistic is whether Jordan is a Palestinian state waiting to happen. Could it be converted into the Palestinian homeland, ready to receive additional Palestinians from the territories now occupied by Israel, simply by replacing the monarchy with a Palestinian republican government? Is this a plausible and realistic way in which the Palestinian problem might be solved?

Or is Jordan an integrated and cohesive state with a political structure that has deep roots in powerful sectors of the population? Would any attempt to impose a Palestinian government, from inside or outside, lead to civil war (as it did in 1970)?

For most Americans, Jordan seems far away and not very important. The Middle East tends to be whatever is the current focus of conflict on the nightly television news. Pressed for a more durable impression, many might identify Israel and oil as the only aspects of the Middle East that matter. Jordan, to the extent that they are aware of it, is primarily King Hussein, the courageous and very lucky bedouin king. For the Jewish community—Americans who do care about the Middle East—Jordan is one of Israel's Arab enemies, though not the worst of them. Why should it matter to Americans what happens to Jordan?

Americans who follow events in the region more closely have long recognized that the United States has a closer connection with Jordan than with any other Arab state. Since the mid-1950s, when the British reduced their commitment, the United States has been the country on which Jordan has depended most. American officials have developed a close working relationship with the King and his advisers. Private American experts have contributed advice to Jordanian economic and military planning for years.

For much of the last thirty years Washington supplied the financial support that made it possible for the King to hold his kingdom together—the functional equivalent of the earlier British subsidy. In more recent years this has been provided by the wealthy Arab governments, and for other reasons as well, the old intimacy has cooled. Egypt under Sadat tended to replace Jordan as a central player for American policy in the area.

From the Jordanian side, the United States replaced Britain in a personal sense as well. The King and many of his principal advisers, together with thousands of other Jordanians, send their children to school here. Many visit the United States frequently. It is no doubt coincidence, but nonetheless emblematic, that King Hussein's first non-Arab wife was British, while his second (his fourth and present wife, the other two having been Arabs) is an American whom he married in 1978.

The long and close relationship between the two countries is one reason why Jordan matters to the United States. There are more basic ones, however, which were largely responsible for the relationship developing in the first place. Jordan is a country so situated, politically and geographically, that whatever happens to it affects everything else in the region.

Jordan is the classic buffer state, surrounded by more wealthy or more powerful countries: Israel, Syria, Iraq, Saudi Arabia, and Egypt. It is not strong or aggressive enough to threaten them. None of them, however, could easily tolerate having the territory Jordan occupies come under the influence of another neighbor. With Israel in control of Jordan, Syria would feel even more surrounded by a deadly enemy, and Iraq and Saudi Arabia would be alarmed. Israel for its part could not abide having Syrian power extend along the border it now shares with Jordan, nor would Iraq, Saudi Arabia or Egypt welcome such Syrian influence along or closer to their borders.

A breakdown of stability in Jordan would arouse the strongest anxieties in Israel and Syria. Each might be inclined to intervene, but neither could tolerate the other's intervention—a recipe for conflict. The royal families of the Arabian (Persian) Gulf, sitting on their treasure of oil, would be deeply troubled. The Jordanian monarchy, after all, stands between them and the tensions of the Arab-Israeli conflict and between their conservative political systems and the violence and radicalism of the northern Arab world. American interests would be affected, and it would be hard for the United States to remain aloof.

There is another more elusive reason for U.S. interest in Jordan. A group of politically active Jordanians, both Palestinians and East Bankers (the "old Jordanians"), were asked recently what they thought was most important for Americans to understand about their country. With little hesitation they replied that Americans should understand Jordan's role in the long-term struggle for the soul of the Arab world. The region, they said, is in the process of being shaped into new forms, old forms having failed to one degree or another. Perhaps it will take its new configuration by the year 2000, perhaps later. Jordan is important as a force in this shaping process. Its generally free economic system, its moderation in religion, its liberal social contract between ruler and citizen are rare in the Arab world. Without Jordan these qualities would have far less chance to impress themselves on the future of the region.

These Jordanians make an important point. Even those Americans who do not follow foreign affairs closely are aware that violence and extremism are a growing threat to them and the kind of world they want to live in. Nowhere has this been clearer than in the Middle East; Lebanon has become a tragic example of a world given over to unbridled violence. Hashemite Jordan is one of the few counterexamples, certainly in the Middle East, of a moderate and civilized state.

In more immediate terms, Jordan matters because the Arab-Israeli conflict matters to the United States. Despite occasional Washington efforts to distance itself from this issue, new flare-ups of tension or violence compel engagement. The Arab-Israeli conflict means the Palestinian problem. And here Jordan is inextricably involved. More than half its population is Palestinian, and the population of the Israeli-occupied West Bank has Jordanian citizenship as well. Even leaving aside the more extreme developments suggested earlier, what happens to the Palestinians happens to Jordan, just as it happens to Israel. Jordan, Israel, and the Palestinians are in a sense handcuffed together. When one twitches the others feel it. And the United States feels it, given its stake in Israel and in the region as a whole.

On the Arab side, Jordan offers the best hope for a solution to the Palestinian problem, or at least for its peaceful management. A solution cannot be reached without the participation of the Palestinians themselves. But, left to their own devices, the Palestinians—with no leadership but the faction-ridden exile groups that make up the Palestine Liberation Organization (PLO)—cannot organize and pursue effective negotiations. The Jordanian government cannot substitute for the Palestinians, but it just may be able to pull and prod them into a negotiating position to which Israel can relate.

Jordan's participation is necessary for an even more basic reason: one of the few aspects of the Palestinian problem on which Israelis agree is that an independent Palestinian state in the West Bank and Gaza is unacceptable. If any of this territory is ever to be returned to Arab control, the Jordanians will almost certainly have to be involved in some way. Jordan is, thus, a necessary participant in any negotiation.

Americans may ask whether King Hussein could not produce a

solution to the problem by turning Jordan over to the Palestinians. The chapters that follow attempt to answer this and other questions by considering the extent to which the monarchy today is an integral part of a modern and cohesive state. Is the modernization process creating strains in a country run by a paternalistic monarch? In thinking about the monarchy it is important to ask whether the country's moderation and Western orientation are inherently Jordanian or reflect the rule of its Hashemite kings. We must also ask whether East Bank-Palestinian relationships are likely to lead to instability. The durability of the Jordanian state as well as the army and its loyalties are other pieces of the puzzle. Will a sagging economy bring social and political tensions that could put the monarchy and the country's cohesion under strain?

Americans have seen other friendly, conservative countries transformed by revolutionary pressures into hostile adversaries. Iran is merely the latest example. With what policies can Washington best protect the American stake in Jordan and its regional role? A final chapter will offer specific suggestions about U.S. policy toward Jordan and how the United States may help—or hurt—the prospects for stability and cohesion there.

Note: Throughout this book the name of Jordan will be used to refer to the territory east of the Jordan River only. The lands on the west bank of the river, which were incorporated into Jordan in 1948 but have been occupied by Israel since 1967, will be referred to as the West Bank. These designations are for practical purposes only.

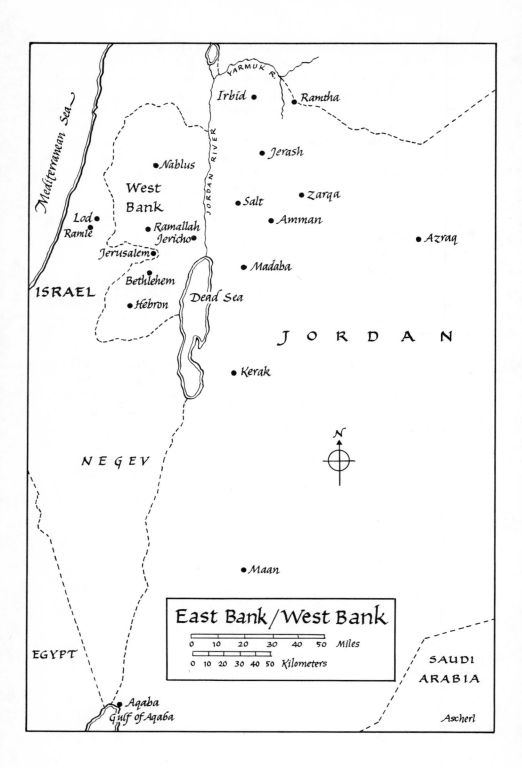

Mediterranean Sea

YARMUK R.

Irbid • •Ramtha

•Jerash

•Nablus

West
Bank

JORDAN RIVER

•Salt •Zarqa

•Amman

Lod •
Ramle •

•Ramallah
Jericho•

•Azraq

Jerusalem •

ISRAEL

Bethlehem•

•Madaba

•Hebron Dead Sea

JORDAN

•Kerak

N

NEGEV

•Maan

East Bank/West Bank

0   10   20   30   40   50   Miles

0 10 20 30 40 50   Kilometers

EGYPT

SAUDI
ARABIA

•Aqaba
Gulf of Aqaba

Ascherl

1

The Land and the Family

N ear the center of Amman, on the flanks of one of the city's many hills, is a quiet park. A road winds through pines and oleander. Set among the trees, hidden from one another, are royal homes the Hashemites have built for themselves since coming here in 1921. They are modest buildings, as palaces go, less impressive than some of the homes the newly rich are putting up on the outskirts of town. The most palatial is Abdallah's palace from the 1920s, with its greater scale and Arabic arches, but it is little used today.

King Hussein lives in Nadwa Palace, smaller and newer, a low, white building with clean lines. It was built for his uncle Emir Nayef in the 1970s. Since coming to the throne in 1952 Hussein has had a number of homes, in this park and elsewhere near Amman, a different one, it seems, with each of his four wives. He describes in his autobiography[1] setting up housekeeping with his second wife, Muna, in a house ten miles from Amman—a house, he emphasizes, that he owned himself as distinct from those owned by the government.

Just above Nadwa Palace is the former headquarters of the British Resident, who wielded such influence on affairs in the early days. It is now an office building for the palace staff. The Resident's home is now the home of Crown Prince Hassan, the King's brother and heir to the throne. His staff has modern office quarters nearby.

The park seems remote from the city outside. It could be the quiet

---

[1]Hussein, King of Jordan, *Uneasy Lies the Head* (New York: Bernard Geis Associates, 1961), p. 304.

campus of a small liberal arts college. The city is not so distant as it appears, however. A small town when Abdallah built his palace near what was then its center, it has grown up around the sides of the park and laps at the foot of the hill. Glimpsed through the oleander, across a narrow valley, is a facing hillside—Jebel et Taj—dense with lower-class houses. Traffic noise from the busy thoroughfares in the valley intrudes on the tranquility. The security arrangements also belie the sense of remote calm. Seen from the valley road, a line of watchtowers runs through the trees a little way up the slope, joined by a continuous fence. Here and there a uniformed figure stands in the undergrowth below the fence. On its far side the park abuts a military installation. A visit to the palace involves clearance through the main gate, at the foot of the hill, manned by a wary detail of Royal Guards, a special select army unit. With their lean faces and hawk-like profiles, they are said to be mostly bedouin, still the most trusted element in the population.

These royal precincts are a good place to begin. The country that the King rules from here is shaped in his image and that of his Hashemite grandfather Abdallah. Its very existence owes much to the ambition and sense of destiny that have driven this singular family, bringing it out of Arabia in the chaotic days after World War I to take over some unpromising real estate and make a nation of it.

The Land

Jordan is not a big country. You can drive the length of it—some 270 miles—from north to south in not much more time than it takes to drive from New York City to Boston. From east to west through central Jordan is a shorter trip. But these miles are important ones in the history of the region and at present.

Driving east from the capital city of Amman one passes at first through farmland. In the early summer, machines are harvesting the grain, and sheep and goats are being let in to graze on the stubble. But within half an hour one is in the desert, at first increasingly barren sand and then suddenly, just beyond the town of Azraq, black volcanic rock that extends to the horizon. Beyond the horizon is more desert, 600 miles of it due east to the Tigris and Euphrates River valleys in Iraq, and angling toward the south, 1,500 miles of it to the Arabian Sea.

If you drive to the west from Amman, the road after a short time winds down the slope of a steep escarpment to the deepest valley in the world. It is a drop of three-quarters of a mile to the Jordan River valley, 1,300 feet below sea level. The air there is heavy and dense. There are scattered trees and houses where water is close to the surface. Irrigated farming is well developed in some sections, with plastic greenhouses glistening in the sun. But during the summer most of the valley floor is parched and barren. The Jordan River itself—the border between Jordan and the Israeli-occupied West Bank—is a muddy little stream flowing through rank undergrowth, surely a disappointment to the pilgrims who revere it for its biblical association. The Dead Sea is a little to the south, out of sight of the road as it approaches the bridge across the Jordan, known to Jordanians as the Hussein Bridge and to the Israelis as the Allenby Bridge, after the British commander in Palestine in World War I, General Sir Edmund Allenby. The bridge is narrow and functional, manned on one end by Jordanian, on the other by Israeli soldiers. Today, getting through the formalities at the two checkpoints can take more time than driving straight from Amman to Jerusalem. Back from the bridge, Israel has a complex of sheds and parking lots that resembles a large truck stop in the United States, and it can take hours, even days, for Arab trucks to negotiate the checks. But once past them, it is a short drive through the oasis town of Jericho and up the slopes to Jerusalem, about the same altitude as Amman. From Jerusalem at night can be seen the lights of Tel Aviv on the Mediterranean coast, about 35 crow-flight miles farther west.

The trip from Amman, leaving aside the checkpoints, has taken less than two hours. From the desert beyond Amman to the sea would take perhaps three and a half hours. That is the distance from one world to another, but it is a trip that has been made by unnumbered thousands throughout history. Moses brought his people that way after their wanderings to cross into Canaan at Jericho. He himself is said to have died without making the crossing. He saw the promised land, however, from Mount Nebo, south of Amman on the rim of the valley, a haze of distant hills, green in winter, an almost incandescent pale brown in summer, with the Dead Sea glinting in the valley below.

The north-south route through Jordan begins at the city of Ramtha, just inside the border with Syria. For most of the way to Amman, an hour and a half away, the road runs through hills. This is farmland and quite heavily populated. Throughout the trip the deep trench of the Jordan valley is on the right, to the west, and the desert is on the left. Neither is far away, for the habitable highlands that constitute the heart of the country are a narrow belt. In the south the desert comes in on the rim of the valley, erasing the fertile highlands altogether.

South of Amman the land flattens out as the road passes the new Queen Alia International Airport. A somewhat unexpected roadsign with the one word "Mecca" confirms that this is the old pilgrimage route. At about this point the Hejaz railway swings in from the east on its way from Istanbul to the holy city of Medina in the Hejaz. It follows the road as far as Maan. The land becomes drier. About a third of the way down the desert asserts itself, rocky and bare; this is, after all, the Desert Highway. At Maan, a desert crossroads town for hundreds of years, the road branches. One branch goes southeast to Saudi Arabia and Mecca; the other turns west, quickly running out of the desert as it drops to the port town of Aqaba on an arm of the Red Sea—the Gulf of Aqaba to Jordan, the Gulf of Eilat to Israel. Eilat is the Israeli town just across the head of the Gulf from Aqaba.

This too is a trip that has been made, in both directions, by armies, caravans and nomads through the millennia. This ancient road, together with the parallel Kings' Highway in the Jordan valley and the coastal road on the Mediterranean, links Syria and Mesopotamia in the north with Egypt and the Red Sea in the south.

It is still an important route. Convoys of great tank trucks are all along it, parked beside the road or moving nose to tail, carrying oil from Iraq to the ships in Aqaba, returning empty for another load. With Iraq's own ports blocked by the war with Iran, this old route provides an important access to the outside world.

For much of its history the stretch of land that Jordan now occupies has been mainly a way of getting somewhere, a path between power centers, the border between adjoining worlds. But it has also at times had identity of its own. In biblical times it consisted of the small states of Gilead, Ammon, Moab and Edom. Amman was then known as Rabbath-Ammon, referred to in records as early as 1300 B.C. as a town controlling the Desert Highway.

Alexander the Great introduced in the fourth century B.C. a long period of Greek influence and prosperity. In 250 B.C. a prominent Greek from Egypt, one Ptolemy Philadelphia, captured the city of Amman and, it is recorded, beautified it, naming it then after himself—Philadelphia. The earlier Semitic name reasserted itself eventually, however, and the town became, and remained, Amman.

Before Alexander, as early as the sixth century B.C., an Arab people—the Nabateans—appeared in the area. They ultimately established an empire astride the caravan routes; they coexisted with the Greeks and even, for a considerable period, with the Romans. At the height of their power, they exercised control over an empire stretching to Damascus and the Euphrates. Their capital was the extraordinary city of Petra, carved into the rose-red cliffs of the Jordan valley between Amman and Aqaba.

Rome gradually asserted itself in the last century of the pre-Christian era. Under Roman rule the country was more populous and prosperous than it has since been until the present day. Amman grew to cover seven hills, a size it did not achieve again until well after World War II. The country was Christianized and during the early Byzantine period Christian towns flourished. Some of their ruins are still evident today, notably the mosaic floors of ancient Christian churches in the town of Madaba. Beginning in the fifth century as Roman power ebbed, the area declined. Some of the cities lay empty, and even Amman was described by a traveler in the nineteenth century as "deserted, with its buildings used for sheepfolds."

During the period of Turkish supremacy from the fifteenth to the nineteenth centuries, this stretch of land ceased to have any separate identity. Most of what is now Jordan was the southern part of Syria, though divided among several administrative districts. The far south of present-day Jordan with the port of Aqaba was the northern tip of the Hejaz, the ancestral home of the Hashemites.

In the chaos that followed defeat of the Ottoman Turks in World War I, the area was distinguished by not being included definitively in any of the jurisdictions being set up by the victors: Syria, Lebanon, Iraq or Palestine. Abdallah, ultimately to be King of Jordan, arrived on the scene in late 1920 as the British were facing the necessity of providing for the administration of the territory.

The Hashemites and the Founding of Jordan

Who Abdallah was, and how he happened to get off a train of the Hejaz railway in the town of Maan in November 1920, is a story that begins back in the time of the Prophet Mohammed in the Hejaz, the land north of Yemen on the Red Sea coast. It is an excursion worth making, to examine the roots of the Hashemite dynasty that has been and still is the central organizing factor in Jordan's life.

The Hejaz is a rugged strip of land along the Red Sea coast across from Egypt and northern Sudan. It is somewhat more than 800 miles long and perhaps 200 miles wide. A band of jagged mountains parallels the coast in a great escarpment that gives the country its name (Hejaz means "barrier" in Arabic). To the west, between the mountains and the sea, lie Mecca and Medina, the holiest cities of Islam. To the east, the inland slopes of the mountains merge into the great desert that stretches on across the Arabian peninsula. The Hejaz is the land into which the Prophet Mohammed was born about 1400 years ago, in the city of Mecca. It was the home of the Qureish, a prosperous tribe that efficiently controlled the caravan trade through the region. Mohammed was a member of the House of Hashem, a subdivision of the Qureish named after his great-grandfather, Amr Hashem.

Mecca was even then a sacred place to the pagan beliefs of that time. The little temple of the Kaaba, the black stone now so sacrosanct to Muslims, was already a local shrine. As Mohammed began to preach the new and more rigorous faith of Islam, however, he ran afoul of the wealthy Qureish merchant-managers who ruled Mecca and they drove him from the city. In 622 A.D., the year from which the calendar of Islam begins counting, Mohammed established his capital at Medina, several hundred miles to the north.

Mohammed left no male heir when he died in 632. The struggle for leadership of the Islamic world, and indeed for the identification of the true Islamic faith, has continued on through the centuries. More locally, and of more relevance to Jordan's history, a struggle ensued also for the rule of the Hejaz and the guardianship of Mecca. Eventually the descendants of Fatima, Mohammed's daughter, and her husband Ali, established themselves as the hereditary emirs (prince is a rough English equivalent) of Mecca. This line became known as *sharifs*—the sharifian family—meaning that they could trace their descent in a direct line from the Prophet (sharif is a form of the Arabic word for descendant).

One of the families that claimed such descent was that of the Hashemites. From the thirteenth century onward they played, with some interruptions, the dual role of guardians of Mecca and Kings of the Hejaz.

It is through Abdallah (Abdallah ibn Hussein ibn Ali ibn Abdal Muin of the dhawi Awn branch of the Hashemite family of the House of Qureish) that the history of this sharifian family becomes the history of Jordan. By Hashemite reckoning, Abdallah was the thirty-eighth generation from the Prophet. He was born in 1882, one of four sons of Sharif Hussein ibn Ali. His brothers were Ali, who was to become the last of his line to rule the Hejaz, Feisal, later King of Iraq, and Zeid, who did not want to be King and who ultimately accompanied his father into exile.

Sharif Hussein is known to the West as the leader of the Arab revolt against the Ottoman Empire during World War I. The revolt itself, however, was the expression of a profound ambition that had been maturing in Hussein's mind for some years before the war. It was an ambition founded in a sense of manifest destiny that carried the Hashemite family to three kingships and that continues to inform the policy of Hussein's namesake and great grandson, the present King of Jordan.

The Ottoman Sultan had detained Sharif Hussein in Constantinople in a form of political exile from his home in the Hejaz during his early manhood. In 1908 the office of Grand Sharif of Mecca became vacant through the death of a Hashemite uncle, and Hussein successfully importuned the Sultan to permit him to take up the post. Returning to the historic domains of his family, Hussein set about restoring the powers and perquisites of the office. It being a time of revolutionary ferment in the Arab world, he also established contact with the secret societies that sprouted in Syria, Egypt and in Turkey itself in opposition to repressive Ottoman rule. He began to think in terms of independence for the Arab world. As the thought took root, it seemed only natural to him that leadership of the Arabs would be vested in the first sharifian family, rulers of Mecca and Guardians of the Holy Places of Islam, and in himself as Grand Sharif. That this assumption was not shared by a great many other Arabs did not deter the Hashemites then and has not done so since.

This sense of family mission took shape in the setting of Arab nationalism, or pan-Arabism, a concept attractive to the Arabs in theory but elusive in practice. It had as its intellectual underpinnings the revival of interest in the Arabic language and literature in the late nineteenth century, sparked in part by Western educators and missionaries in the Levant. In time, it spread to wider Arab circles and broadened to a cultural and political nationalism.

World War I provided the impetus for Arab nationalism to move from abstract hope to the stage of practical reality, or so it seemed. Oblique and complex negotiations (beginning, in fact, before the war) between the Grand Sharif and British officials in Cairo led in 1916 to an agreement for Hussein to lead an Arab revolt in return for carefully qualified British undertakings to establish Arab independence in a large part—but not all—of the Arab world after the war. The Grand Sharif would be king of this independent Arab land. In November of that year Hussein had himself proclaimed King of the Arab Countries, a title that found, however, no echo outside his capital in Mecca.

Once the war ended the Hashemite vision faded in the hard realities of the peace. Britain and France divided the fertile crescent of northern Arab lands into colonial holdings in the form of League of Nations mandates. France acquired Syria and Lebanon; Britain took over Iraq and Palestine.

The area that was to become Jordan was left in limbo. It became part of Occupied Enemy Territory (OET) under the British, and British, Australian and Indian troops remained until the end of 1919. It was assigned by the British OET order to the military jurisdiction of the short-lived Arab government established in Syria by Abdallah's brother Feisal. Feisal was chased out of Damascus by the French in 1920, however, and a year later became King of Iraq. The territory slipped back into local rule by towns and tribes. The Majali tribe in the town of Kerak, for example, set up a "Moabite Arab Government" presided over by one of the British officials who had somehow re-mained on the scene, Alec Kirkbride by name, who was for the next thirty years associated with Abdallah as British Resident and subse-quently ambassador in Amman.

In August 1920 the British High Commissioner of Palestine, Sir Herbert Samuel, told an assemblage of notables gathered in the Trans-jordanian town of Salt that the British did not want to incorporate Transjordan into the Palestine administration, despite its mandatory responsibility for the area. Britain therefore intended to set up separate administrations in the major towns. In this highly anarchical atmos-phere, numbers of Syrian nationalists who had fled south after the French took over Damascus awaited leadership to take them back to Syria.

Abdallah had spent the last years of the war pinning down Turk-ish troops in the Medina area, and he now languished in Mecca with-out a significant role to play. It was a low point in his career. A Saudi force had badly defeated him in 1919, costing him prestige among the tribes and creating tensions with his father. He was envious of his younger brother Feisal, playing an active if ultimately futile part on the grand stage of the peace talks in Europe.

In the autumn of 1920, he recounts in his memoirs, supporters of the Arab cause in Syria requested that a member of the Hashemite family be sent to take the place of Feisal. By his account, he obtained his father's approval to go in response to this appeal, and without delay headed north toward Syria. Some say the initiative was his own, and that he sought an outlet for his ambition in more promising surround-ings. He made his way north to Maan on the Hejaz railway, stopping at frequent intervals to have trees cut down for fuel, and arrived in November. A few months later, on March 1, 1921, he went on to Amman where he was welcomed by the Syrian nationalists but found little enthusiasm for the cause among local Arabs, who put a price on their participation.

The British could see nothing ahead but trouble. If their territory was used as a staging ground for attacks on the French Mandate in Syria, there would be continuing friction with France. They decided to make the best of Abdallah's presence by offering him rule over the awkward piece of territory in which he found himself, east of the Jordan River and south of Syria. They would thus, in one stroke, provide a nucleus of control and authority for the area and also induce Abdallah to forgo his Syrian adventure. Winston Churchill, Colonial Secretary at the time, was in Cairo for a conference on British Middle East policy that settled all important aspects except Transjordan. Churchill shifted the conference to Jerusalem, in effect, and pursued the subject there with Abdallah.

There is a photograph showing Abdallah during the Jerusalem conference of March 1921. He stands on the steps of an unidentified building in Jerusalem between Sir Herbert Samuel and Mrs. Samuel, with Churchill, Mrs. Churchill and a scattering of Arab military officers. He is in Western military uniform, though with flowing Arab headdress. A small man, he holds himself very erect among larger people. His diminutive stature brings to mind Hussein, the present King, and his brother, Crown Prince Hassan, both also short men. In other respects, however, Abdallah in these early pictures does not resemble Hussein. His face is rounder with a foxy expression while Hussein is marked by a direct, level gaze. Another photograph shows him more clearly as an Arab leader: standing in front of a World War I airplane with Samuel and T. E. Lawrence, he is all flowing robes and headdress, his hand folded over the ceremonial dagger at his waist, squinting slightly into the sun.

Churchill persuaded Abdallah to abandon a hopeless Syrian enterprise and accept the title of Emir of Transjordan. By then Abdallah had, in fact, largely put aside the liberation of Syria as impracticable and had begun to establish himself in Amman. He was appointed Emir on April 11, 1921. The British kept Transjordan separate from their Palestine Mandate, to be developed as an Arab principality.

As the Hashemites now took over Transjordan and Iraq (where Feisal assumed his throne in June 1921), the centuries-old family connection with the Hejaz and the Muslim holy cities was coming to an end. Rivalries among tribal leaders in the Arabian peninsula had intensified with the end of the war, among them the hostility between ibn Saud, Sultan of Nejd, and Sharif Hussein of the Hejaz. Saud commanded the loyalties of the Wahabis, a fierce desert sect of rigorous Islamic persuasion, and was far more powerful than Hussein, who then in any case was in his declining years. Saudi anger was aroused when Hussein had the poor judgment, in 1924, to declare himself Caliph—head of the world Muslim community—after the Turks had abolished the office and dismissed the incumbent. Ibn Saud and his Wahabis swept down on the Hejaz and Hussein abdicated in favor of his son Ali, sailing away to Aqaba on the old Red Sea steamer, *The Two Mercies*.

Before long Ali too was forced out, and the Hejaz became part of Saudi Arabia. In the last days of his rule, Ali, on British urging, transferred the Hejaz cities of Aqaba and Maan to Transjordan. With this addition, and another adjustment made in the same period that extended Transjordanian territory eastward to the Iraqi border, the country's boundaries took the shape they were to have until 1948. As for Ali, he lived out his life in Iraq under the watchful eye of his Hashemite relatives.

Abdallah's Reign

It would be an unnecessary diversion to recount Abdallah's reign in detail. Three major themes of his period, however, have continued to be important in that of his grandson Hussein: establishing legitimacy and consolidating power; devising a mix of paternalism and popular representation in government; and pursuing the Hashemite sense of family destiny and a broader role in the Arab world.

Abdallah's first task was to establish his authority over the diverse groups making up his new emirate. The British had already created a small military force under a British captain from the Egyptian Camel Corps, Frederick G. Peake, to back up the local police in places where the few British officials were operating. After the Emir took over and persuaded the British to support a unit of 750 men, Peake became commander of a force known as the Arab Legion. It remained effectively under British control, an arrangement that was to persist throughout Abdallah's reign into that of Hussein.

The Legion was composed at that time of Arabs from the defeated Ottoman armies and from Egypt and elsewhere outside the emirate. Maintaining control over such a fractious force was a problem in itself.

But the principal challenge to British authority and that of Abdallah came from the bedouin tribes that carried on their tradition of intertribal conflict and raiding. There were three main camel-breeding tribes (the elite in the tribal hierarchy, the tribes that kept sheep and goats being lower on the scale) entirely within Transjordan: the Bani Saqr southeast of Amman, the Huweitat in the far south, and the Sirhan in the north. There were many lesser tribes as well, and some that passed in and out of the country through tribal territories that lay across the new boundaries. Peake's force, seen by these tribes as alien and hostile, met little success in bringing order.

A new tactic was brought into play by another British officer, transferred from Iraq in 1930. John Bagot Glubb had worked for ten years with the bedouin tribes there, and in Transjordan he organized a force—the Desert Mobile Force—composed largely of bedouin. He coopted the tribes, in effect, by giving them a vested interest in the force. In so doing he established as well the identification of the bedouin army with its leader and ultimately with the monarch, an identification that has been a major factor in Hashemite rule until today. Glubb himself, known as Glubb Pasha, commanded the force, which eventually merged with the Arab Legion, until 1956.

Another pattern emerged at that time which endured into Hussein's reign. The population in the south of the emirate was heavily tribal, with strong ties to the Arabian peninsula including Abdallah's ancestral home, the Hejaz. They spoke the dialect of that region. In the north, the population was settled, speaking a Syrian dialect and attuned to Syrian and Palestinian ideas and interests. Abdallah won the loyalty of the south and based his rule on it. Although he could not establish himself so firmly in the north, he could afford to ignore the resistance he encountered there.

Not all the threats to Abdallah's reign came from within. The Saudis, in their mounting campaign against the Hashemites, raided Transjordan from the deserts to the south in 1922 and on a larger scale in 1924. The raids were beaten back by the Arab Legion with the help in 1924 of four armored cars and two airplanes of the British Royal Air Force. The legitimacy of Abdallah's new rule was enhanced by his ability to protect his emirate from outside attack.

The political aspects of the Emir's rule gradually took shape during the same period. The instruments of government seemed to fall into two parts: an informal, personal process of government that derived from local practice; and trappings of constitutional government that derived from Western experience.

The Emir maintained wide contacts with the settled and nomadic tribes. He kept an open-house one day a week—on Friday—on the order of the traditional *majlis* of Arab rulers. Anyone could drop in and complain or discuss with Abdallah what was on his mind.

The formal structure did not fall into place so easily, partly because the British retained effective control and did not intend to permit democratic institutions to arise that would have genuine power. An executive council of leading citizens functioned as a sort of advisory cabinet for the Emir, though it had no power. The continuing bone of contention was the creation of some form of legislature. A small group of town dwellers—educated, middle class professionals for the most part, in tune with Arab nationalism, mainly from the towns in the north and not basically well-disposed toward the regime—agitated throughout the 1920s for elected democratic institutions and an end to the British role. This pattern was to repeat itself over succeeding decades.

A legislative council, which the British pruned into a rubber-stamp, was eventually set up. The Anglo-Jordanian treaty of 1928, which recognized the emirate as independent with some retained British powers, was accompanied by an Organic Law that provided for a Legislative Council. This was formally established in 1929 but was indirectly elected, had little power, and did not last long. When it refused to approve a budget, Abdallah dissolved it, a recourse that also became a familiar aspect of Hashemite rule.

A treaty with the British in March 1946 made Transjordan a nominally independent state—the Hashemite Kingdom of Transjordan. In May Abdallah became king but the British retained control of the Arab Legion and provided a substantial annual subsidy. The continuing British connection so compromised the kingdom's status that many countries did not recognize its independence, and the Soviet Union blocked its admission to the United Nations. The United States held off recognition until 1949, after the armistice that ended the first Arab-Israeli war. The country was admitted to the United Nations in 1954. The name Transjordan was dropped in favor of Jordan when the West Bank was incorporated into the kingdom after the 1947–49 war.

Though he was forced to settle for the principality of Transjordan, Abdallah, more than any of his brothers, continued to cherish the Hashemite ambition for a greater destiny. Throughout his life he proposed again and again the establishment of a Greater Syria under his rule. On one occasion he called for a Syrian constituent assembly to establish a union of Syria, Transjordan and Palestine.

More immediately, he kept a covetous eye on Mandate Palestine across the Jordan River. He could not in any case entirely ignore the stormy developments of the Mandate years as the Palestinian Arabs resisted Jewish immigration and as Arab factions struggled among themselves for advantage. The ties between the two banks of the Jordan River were too close for the Emir not to be concerned about these events even had he not entertained the ambition to expand his realm westward one day. The Arab riots of 1936 in Palestine against Jewish immigration aroused especially strong public feeling in Transjordan, though Abdallah maintained a strict neutrality.

Palestine attracted Abdallah in his desert capital as a far richer territory with its extensive farmlands, prosperous cities, and active trade. It was also a vastly more important stage for his ambitions, containing as it did Jerusalem—a world religious center and the third holiest city in Islam after the two his family had lost in the Hejaz. The Emir was wary of involving himself with Palestine, however, because of British control there. By the late 1930s, as London began exploring the idea of partitioning Palestine between Arabs and Jews, he saw that his hopes for expansion might fit in with British plans.

In the late 1930s and especially during the early 1940s, therefore, he worked to build political support for himself across the Jordan River. He wanted to strengthen the moderate forces, represented by such families as the Nashashibis and the Tuqans, against his bitter adversaries, the Husseinis, led by the redoubtable Haj Amin, Mufti of Jerusalem. The Mufti saw himself, not Abdallah, as the logical and rightful ruler of Arab Palestine.

As the British Mandate drew to an end in 1947 and 1948, Abdallah's involvement in Palestine and with its future became more urgent. The November 1947 United Nations Resolution providing for partition of Palestine between Arabs and Jews crystallized the issue. Not only did the opportunity for expansion of his realm become more tangible, but the dangers of allowing his enemies—in the first instance the Husseinis—to take control in Arab Palestine after British departure became more real as well.

Abdallah supported the partition resolution, the only Arab leader to do so, seeing himself as the heir to the Arab portion of a partitioned Palestine, an inheritance Britain encouraged. During negotiations with the British in 1948 over a final treaty putting the London-Amman relationship on a durable footing, it was agreed that Jordanian forces would occupy the areas of Palestine designated for the Arabs by the resolution when the British withdrew.

British withdrawal on May 15, 1948, touched off the anticipated conflict. There had, in fact, been sporadic fighting for several months between Jewish and Palestinian Arab elements maneuvering for what both knew would be a race to take over territory in the wake of British departure. On May 15 the forces of neighboring Arab states joined in. Their avowed aim was the defeat of Jewish forces and the preservation of the entire country for the Palestinians. Abdallah, for his part, clearly had the intention of staying in Palestine, but the military outcome of the war made the distinction moot in any case.

The Jewish leadership, just before the Mandate expired, made a last-minute effort to persuade Abdallah to keep out of the impending fighting. A Jewish delegation under Golda Myerson (later Golda Meier) visited the King secretly with this aim. Abdallah, who would have preferred a peaceful way out of the dispute, found himself boxed in by the determination throughout the Arab world to crush the Jewish state at birth. There was no agreement.

The Arab Legion, together with a small Iraqi unit, moved across the Jordan River into the West Bank on the morning of May 15, occupying most of it. The Legion also pushed down out of the West Bank hills, along the Jerusalem-Tel Aviv road, to occupy a finger of land that included the important towns of Ramle and Lydda (site of Israel's international airport). At about the same time, the Egyptians advanced from the south, and the Syrians and Lebanese moved across the northern borders.

The Arabs made good progress at first, but as truces came and went, and Israel strengthened its forces, the tide turned. By mid-January of 1949 Israel had occupied substantially all of Palestine except for the West Bank, held by Jordan, and a small area along the southern coast known as the Gaza Strip, held by Egypt. Only the Jordanian troops had held their ground, though they had been forced to abandon Ramle and Lydda. Following the Arab Legion's retreat from these towns, the Israelis drove out the inhabitants, and Palestinians long harbored great bitterness at being, as they saw it, sold out by the British-commanded Legion. Early in 1949, with the armistice talks already in progress on the island of Rhodes, Abdallah was forced by the Israelis to surrender a further strip of land along the western flank of the West Bank, depriving many West Bank farmers of their fields. Palestinian bitterness against King Abdallah was deepened further.

The political drama of Jordanian annexation of the West Bank was played out some months earlier when most of the fighting had already ended. Knowing of Abdallah's intention to annex the territory, which his troops largely controlled, the Arab League moved in September 1948 to head him off. It established an All-Palestinian Government under the Mufti of Jerusalem, located in the Gaza Strip, to be the legitimate spokesman for the Palestinians and the government of all of Palestine including the West Bank.

Abdallah maneuvered quickly to organize a Palestinian Congress of his supporters, which was held in Amman on October 1. The Congress repudiated the Gaza government and petitioned Abdallah to take Arab Palestinians under his protection. Two months later, in December, a large gathering of West Bank notables for the most part friendly to Abdallah was held in the West Bank town of Jericho. The Arab Legion provided transport for participants, and various other inducements were employed to produce a favorable result. The conference issued a formal call for union of the West Bank and Jordan. The Jordanian cabinet in due course approved.

This time the Hashemites were successful in asserting their primacy over an indigenous Palestinian leadership supported by the Arab League. Thirty-six years later the wheel was to come full circle at an Arab summit in Rabat, when the representation of Palestinian interests was officially taken from Jordan and vested in Yasir Arafat's Palestine Liberation Organization (PLO).

After the dust settled, the Jordanians held elections on both East and West Banks in April 1950 to choose a new lower house of the Jordanian Parliament representing both banks. The King appointed an upper house of twenty members, seven of whom were West Bankers. The new Parliament met and endorsed the union. The deed was done. Jordan had irrevocably become a part of the Palestine problem.

In one stroke Abdallah had transformed his kingdom. The old East Bank population of Transjordan was now overwhelmed by a new majority of Palestinians, many of them refugees. Numbers tell much of the story. Prior to the merger, Transjordan had a population of little more than 430,000. By 1950 almost twice this many Palestinians had been added, more than 850,000. The total population of Jordan, as the merged state was called, was virtually triple that of Transjordan: more than 1,280,000, of whom almost two-thirds were Palestinians.

The 850,000 Palestinians fell into two broad categories. About 400,000 were indigenous residents of the West Bank who stayed in their own towns and villages as they came under Jordanian control. A larger number, 450,000, were refugees who had fled from the area taken over by Israel (this was the number of refugees officially designated by the United Nations agency set up to care for them, UNRWA, but there were additional thousands who fled without benefit of such designation). Some fled into the West Bank and found places to live in the towns there or were assembled into camps; some of the well-to-do from cities along the coast had summer places in the hills, which now became their homes. Others came directly across the Jordan River to the East Bank, followed by increasing numbers in succeeding years.

The refugees who found themselves under Jordanian rule in 1948 were understandably far from happy with their new situation. In their political relationship with Jordan they were torn by two conflicting aims. Most of them at first resisted absorption into the new state because they wanted to emphasize their determination ultimately to return to their former homes. There was much debate among them on, for example, whether to participate as candidates or even to vote in the 1950 parliamentary elections.

At the same time, they wanted to move Jordanian policy toward a more militant irredentism. They believed that Jordan was too ready to reach accommodation with Israel at their expense. In part they blamed this on continuing British influence through British command of the Arab Legion, and they agitated for Jordan to free itself of this link. Thus, while some Palestinians were boycotting the elections, others were pressing for increased representation in Parliament to reflect their majority, rather than dividing the seats half and half with East Bank Jordanians.

Abdallah was assiduous in his efforts to win support of some leading Palestinian families. Those that had backed his annexation of the West Bank were liberally rewarded with prominent positions in the Jordanian government. Family representatives were elected to the lower house of Parliament and appointed to the upper house. Some members of the Nusseibeh family of Jerusalem, for example, or of the Tuqan family of Nablus, served as ministers in a series of cabinet posts. These posts enabled Palestinian families to give government jobs to their relatives and friends. Some ministries became heavily Palestinian, the Ministry of Foreign Affairs, for instance. Most of Jordan's ambassadors were from the loyalist Palestinian families.

At the popular level, however, dissident political groups flourished among the Palestinians, especially on the West Bank. While they fed on indigenous grievances, all the major political groups originated outside Jordan and maintained close ties beyond the kingdom. They were carefully watched and in some cases suppressed by Abdallah's security forces, but they did not pose a serious political threat at that time. That was to come on Hussein's watch in the late 1950s and 1960s.

The threat that Palestinians posed for Abdallah was of a more personal character. He was denounced throughout the Arab World as a traitor to the Arab cause for annexing the West Bank and for shortly thereafter opening secret negotiations with Israel in a forlorn effort to obtain access for Jordan to the Mediterranean at Haifa. Rumors of plots against his life proliferated, and on June 21, 1951, one plot succeeded. He was shot and killed as he entered El Aksa Mosque, within the sacred precincts of the Haram Sharif in Jerusalem, in the company of his grandson, Hussein. There were many fingers on the trigger. Six Palestinians were sentenced to death for the murder. But the trail of ultimate responsibility led back to associates of the Mufti, Haj Amin, far away in Cairo. Abdallah's loyal troops savaged Jerusalem in their outrage.

Hussein—The Dynasty Continued

Abdallah left two sons by different wives. The elder was Talal. Quiet, withdrawn and suffering from schizophrenia, he was not a promising choice to succeed his father. The younger, Nayef, was not a Hashemite on his mother's side, however, and was not considered seriously as a candidate—except by himself and a circle of supporters. It is said that Talal's wife, Zein, a woman of insight and ability, knowing how serious her husband's mental condition was, wanted her eldest son Hussein to be king. Certainly Abdallah, deeply disappointed in Talal, had felt that Hussein had the makings of a king and had taken great pains to prepare him for this role. A number of voices, including that of the influential British Resident, pressed for Talal's succession, however, and Parliament settled on him. He was crowned almost at once.

Talal's unfitness became quickly apparent as bouts of madness and violence came to public attention. In August 1952 Parliament called on him to abdicate, which he did. In his autobiography,[2] Hussein recounts that he was vacationing with his mother, sisters and brother in Lausanne, Switzerland, in the old Beau Rivage Hotel, when a cablegram from Jordan was brought to him addressed to "His Majesty." Without opening it he knew that his carefree days were over, and indeed they were.

---

[2]*Ibid.*, p. 37.

He was sixteen years old at the time, too young, it was thought, to act as king. He was sent off, therefore, in September for a short course at the British military school of Sandhurst, leaving the Kingdom in the hands of a regency council, and did not take up his royal duties until May 1953 at the age of seventeen.

Hussein was and is a serious, even moody person, self-confident but at the same time subject to feelings of melancholy and loneliness. In his early years he did not mix easily with his classmates in the British schools he attended. Neither sports nor studies came readily to him. Later his love of fast cars and planes and the many women in his life gave him the reputation of being a rich playboy. But he was not frivolous, and he certainly was not rich. Speed seems to relax him. His attraction to women is more complex. He himself, in his early autobiography, speaks again and again of his need for an understanding companion and describes his early years with his second wife, Muna, as a time of happy domesticity. Some who know him, however, speak of Hussein as liking beautiful women, period. No doubt there is truth in both images.

His obvious physical courage, notably displayed at critical points in his reign, coupled with the love of fast driving and flying, gave rise to the impression of a somewhat foolhardy bravery. By now it is clear that his apparent personal recklessness is indeed bravery, but a prudent and calculated bravery made use of at the right times for the right reasons.

In his personal style and appearance he is very much a king. Though short and slight, he is muscular and wiry with a remarkable presence which is enhanced by his deep and melodious voice. He speaks slowly and fixes his interlocutor with a calm and steady gaze. He has a reputation for great charm and courtesy and an altogether royal manner.

Hussein's family life has been important in his reign, especially in the early years. His mother, with her strength and good sense, remained an important influence, together with Sharif Nasser, a Hashemite notable descended from Hussein ibn Ali's family. They provided steadying support during the difficult 1950s and 1960s. He had the strength to assert his own will as he grew in experience, however, and the two eventually came to play less of a role.

The King has had four wives. The first was a distant Hashemite cousin from Cairo, Sharifa Dina Abdul Hamid. He was nineteen at the time, she, considerably older. It was a bad match. She was an intellectual—a bookworm, as one who knew the couple describes her. Hussein is astute and intelligent but not at all an intellectual. He liked to talk about cars and planes, for example, which were not subjects that attracted the interest of Dina with her degree from Cambridge. After eighteen months the family suggested she return to Cairo and she did; a divorce followed shortly.[3]

Hussein's second wife, whom he married in 1961, was a young English woman named Toni Avril Gardiner, daughter of a British military attache in Amman. She was given the Arab name Muna and became a Muslim, but her being English posed a problem nonetheless. She was not made queen, and her oldest son, the King's first male child, is not now the first in line among his children. Hussein and Muna were divorced in 1972.

The third wife, Alia, was from the prominent Tuqan family in Nablus. Although her own immediate family settled in Amman before World War II, the original Palestinian lineage was widely noted when her two children were born. She was killed tragically in a helicopter crash in early 1977, leaving the King in a state of shock and depression for months thereafter. A year and a half later he was married again, to Lisa Halaby, the American-born and -raised daughter of Najeeb Halaby, one-time head of Pan America World Airways. She is now called Queen Noor and has borne the King three children.

The question of the succession has been especially important and troublesome for Hussein and his family. The Hashemites do not have great family depth, as the Saudis do for example, with layers and branches of potential male heirs to buttress the monarchy. When Princess Muna's son Abdallah, Hussein's eldest son, was born, he was welcomed as heir to the throne. Hussein writes of the occasion in his autobiography, published the same year as the child's birth, 1962: he "has provided the throne. . .with a direct heir"; he "is now the crown prince." A postage stamp was issued to that effect. In 1965, however, the King ordered an amendment to the constitution according to which he appointed Hassan, his own younger brother, as crown prince. In 1974, when Ali was born, the first son of an Arab wife—Alia—he was named "successor to the Crown Prince." And that is the arrangement that still obtains.

It is said that the Queen Mother and Sharif Nasser pressed the King to name Hassan in 1965. It was a perilous time for the monarchy

---

[3]Dina is now married to Saleh al-Taamari, a prominent figure in the PLO.

and the country. Prince Abdallah was only three years old, and his mother was non-Arab. Presumably the move was to fortify the Hashemite position even as Hussein ruled by demonstrating that a ready and qualified successor was at hand, and to reduce the chances of faltering in the succession should one of the many attempts on Hussein's life succeed. The family was clearly reaching for the most qualified successor, since Hassan was not the next oldest brother, but the third son of Queen Zein. The second son, mentally unstable, was not considered up to the job.

In recent years the family seems to be giving public exposure to Prince Abdallah, Muna's son and the oldest prince, having him participate in ceremonial events, visits and the like. He is now in his twenties, and the family may feel he can contribute an element of stability and durability to the monarchy.

Hassan is an asset for the monarchy. He complements the King, being of an intellectual and scholarly bent. He followed his elder brother to the British public school of Harrow but then went on to take a degree in oriental studies at Oxford in 1967. He is a prolific writer and speaker, a frequent participant in conferences on a wide range of subjects, and the author of three books on the Palestinian problem. It is said of him that if there is a symposium being held anywhere, he will be sure to be found addressing it.

He is short, like the King, but more stocky. He moves briskly and without the grave bearing of his brother. His rapid and fluent English comes in staccato bursts and complex sentences that are often difficult to follow. His approach to a subject tends toward the ironic, and on the political questions of the Middle East his pessimism contrasts with Hussein's optimistic outlook. A reigning king has to seem optimistic, of course; but in this as in other ways Hassan may well express an aspect of his brother's view that Hussein guards from the public. When it comes to getting something done, however, Hassan can be positive and practical. Since 1971 he has overseen the kingdom's economic development, which is generally considered a model in its effectiveness and use of resources. Hassan is married to an attractive Pakistani, Princess Sarvath; they have four children.

2

Pressures on the Monarchy: Will the Center Hold?

In the first two decades after Abdallah's assassination it seemed many times that the Hashemite vision was coming to an end in Jordan. The monarchy was subjected to the most intense pressures during the 1950s and 1960s. Observers writing about Jordan in those years tended to see Hussein as a tragic figure, a little king who had outlived the age of kings and had at best a few years before the forces of modernity swept him away. He himself, in *Uneasy Lies the Head*, writes of waking up at dawn after a restless night, thinking to himself: "Where will it all end? What's going to happen today?"[1] What happened that day was more often than not trouble. But the King's head, though it lay uneasy, remained in place.

Politics and Attempted Coups

Hussein inherited a Jordan that was becoming highly politicized under pressure from the Palestinians with their greater sophistication and frustrations. By the mid-1950s the country was steeped in politics. Political parties flourished. Some that were officially banned were nonetheless active, especially the Communist Party and the Baath—the Syrian-centered socialist pan-Arab party. Teachers recruited students for rival parties. The personnel of UNRWA—the U.N. agency

---

[1]*Op. cit.*, p. 216.

caring for Palestinian refugees—were actively recruited. Sporting clubs were used by some parties as cover for politics. King Hussein writes: "To find a job in Jordan one had to belong to a party. Even to pass an examination at school one had to belong to a party!"[2]

What gave an especially pernicious cast to the situation was that the political strings were being pulled from outside Jordan. The political parties of that day were "not Jordanian," one senior political figure recalls. That was the heyday of pan-Arabism of a strongly socialist flavor, a philosophy that gave other Arab states ample grounds to intervene in Jordan. The Kingdom was at that early stage of its political development a highly permeable society, susceptible to outside influence. The leadership and ideology of Egypt's Gamal Abdel Nasser seemed to many Jordanians, particularly the Palestinians, to be the revitalizing force that would enable the Arabs to overcome Israel and the oppressive influence of the West. Nasser and his Syrian allies beat a drumroll of propaganda against the Hashemites and their connections with "imperialist Britain," calling for an end to the monarchy and the establishment of a republic.

The cheap transistor radio had arrived on the market, giving a new power to radio propaganda that Nasser exploited fully. With it, he and the Syrian Baath party could bring Jordanians into the streets in clamorous demonstrations against the King and his policies. They did so notably in contesting Hussein's intention in 1955 to join the U.S.- and British-sponsored Baghdad Pact against Soviet expansion in the area. They forced the King to back down. The propaganda against the British connection, which reinforced a long-held bitterness of the Palestinians against British control of the Arab Legion, played an important part in the King's decision to dismiss the British commander of the Legion in 1956.

The government gradually developed a flexible mix of techniques in dealing with this hostile activity. The security services were at first somewhat unprepared for the scope and intensity of it, especially on the West Bank. They soon polished the standard tactics of infiltration, harassment and punishment. Hard-core activists were at times harshly dealt with as examples for others. Students could be expelled from school (threatening their careers), prevented from studying abroad, or denied re-entry after studying abroad. The authorities harrassed and

---

[2]*Ibid.*, p. 166.

hindered opposition parties, imprisoning their members at times, and also promoted parties that would support the government.

The high point of political parties was the election of October 1956; it sticks in the minds of Jordanians even today. It was a free election, as others had not been. Seven parties succeeded in electing at least one deputy. The opposition National Socialist Party, which emerged as the most powerful, represented prominent Palestinians and to some extent East Bankers who had hitherto been excluded from power and who wanted what they considered to be economic and political reforms. While they claimed not to oppose the monarchy as such, they pressed for a constitutional monarchical system in which the King's power would be much reduced. They also strongly supported the policies of Egypt and Syria. The party was led by Suleiman Nabulsi, member of a leading West Bank family. The outcome of the election reflected the fraying of the loyalist coalition of notable West Bank families that Abdallah had put together and that had played a major role in the government since that time.

Nabulsi, as head of the largest Parliamentary faction, was asked to form a government. He did so by bringing smaller and more radical parties into the cabinet. The new government immediately set about shifting Jordan's orientation from its traditional British ties to support of Egypt and Syria. Such a re-alignment was much accelerated by the joint Israeli, French and British attack on Egypt a week after the government took office, bringing out rioting crowds that attacked British installations throughout the country. The treaty with Britain was terminated and with it the British subsidy, ending a relationship of thirty-five years.

During the next few months public agitation died down and the King began to restore his position, initiating confidential contacts with the U.S. government that eventually led to the close and continuing relationship which replaced the British link. At this point, however, in April 1957, events within the government and the army took a sinister turn that brought Hussein very close to losing his throne.

A group of military officers, calling themselves the Free Officers, had formed under the leadership of General Ali Abu Nuwar, newly appointed Chief of Staff. Abu Nuwar was a townsman from Salt who had been a protege of the King's and had been promoted over many more senior officers to lead the army after the dismissal of the British commander, Glubb Pasha, in 1956. The Free Officers set in motion a plot to overthrow the King, drawing in Nabulsi.

The first overt move came on April 8, 1957, when the First Armored Car Regiment suddenly surrounded Amman without the King's knowledge. When Hussein learned of it and queried Abu Nuwar, the answers he received only increased his suspicions that trouble was afoot. The regiment was withdrawn, but the cabinet began ordering the retirement of senior officials loyal to the King, including the Chief of the Royal Court and the Director of Security. This was too much for Hussein, and he dismissed the government on April 10.

Abu Nuwar continued down the same path, however, moving loyal army units out into the desert away from Amman. On April 13 a key artillery regiment was ordered to move but resisted and mutinied. Rumors of the King's death reached the troops, most of whom were loyal bedouin soldiers, and they set out to march on Amman to find out for themselves.

The stage was set for the most dramatic and decisive act of Hussein's reign. Informed of these events by loyal officers, he jumped into an open car with Abu Nuwar and some loyal officers and drove out to see what was going on. When he encountered the troops headed for the capital, and when they found him still alive, they rejoiced wildly and very nearly killed the traitorous Abu Nuwar, whom the King sent back to Amman for his health. Hussein went on to their base at nearby Zarqa. Here he reconstituted some semblance of order and established himself firmly in the military heart. An historian of the Jordanian army comments that "At the tender age of 22, he was the undisputed leader of Jordan."[3]

He was also determined to put an end to the conditions that almost toppled him. Security forces made mass arrests. Abu Nuwar was banished to Syria. Political parties were banned, and martial law was declared. Parliament was suspended for three months, and a number of members, hostile to the monarchy, were eventually forced to resign.

King Hussein was by no means out of the woods, however. Pressures from Cairo and Damascus continued, with Arab unity as the theme. As before, Jordanians went into the streets on behalf of this cause. In the wake of the 1958 coup that overthrew and killed the King's cousin, King Feisal of Iraq, the British sent troops to Jordan to help maintain stability. Hussein once more declared martial law and sent his army to keep order in the streets.

After the 1957 coup attempt, however, through the subsequent

---

[3]Brigadier S.A. El-Edroos, *The Hashemite Arab Army 1908–1979* (Amman, The Publishing Committee, 1980), p. 319.

troubled years, the kingdom was kept on a far tighter rein. Parties operated underground in a cat-and-mouse game with security authorities, but, as one analyst of the period puts it, "it being clearly understood that the regime was to play the cat and the parties the mouse, and not the reverse."[4] Parliamentary elections were held but were more carefully controlled. The leadership did not hesitate to nip trouble in the bud by sending the army to contain public demonstrations.

By the mid-1960s a new cloud appeared on the horizon, destined to become large and dark in short order. An Arab League Council summit meeting in 1964 created the Palestine Liberation Organization (PLO). Shortly thereafter, the Palestinian organization named Fatah, established years before under Yasir Arafat as a political movement, launched its military guerrilla campaign against Israel. Almost at once the two organizations posed serious difficulties for Jordan.

Palestinian raids from Jordanian territory into Israel, bringing Israeli retaliation, had been a problem since 1948, At one period, Egypt had sponsored Palestinian raids in the expectation that the Israeli reprisals would help destabilize the Hashemite regime. The government had generally managed to keep the raiding activity limited, though some damaging Israeli reprisals had occurred. Now the Palestinian organizations stepped up raiding, catching Jordan in a damaging whipsaw. Efforts to turn back the guerrilla operations were regarded as anti-Palestinian. When the raids were not prevented and the Israeli retaliation came, the Jordanian army was criticized for not protecting Palestinian camps and villages, the Israeli targets. Eventually, in 1966, Jordan banned the PLO, an action that, in turn, led to border clashes with the Syrians.

At this point another major fracture line cut across Middle East history. Very little was entirely the same after the six-day Arab-Israeli war of June 1967. With the conquest of the West Bank by Israel, Jordan lost a productive part of its territory, one-third of its population, and the holy city of Jerusalem. The kingdom's economy was hard hit just as it had to absorb 310,000 more refugees who streamed across the Jordan River from the West Bank and Gaza as a result of the war. Many of the refugees were fleeing for the second time, leaving empty behind them the great mud-brick camps in the Jordan valley. The shattering defeat exposed the weakness of the Arab states to their own people and to the Palestinians, who, as usual, bore the brunt of it.

---

[4]Amnon Cohen, *Political Parties in the West Bank Under the Jordanian Regime 1949–1967* (Ithaca: Cornell University Press, 1982), p. 239.

In these circumstances, the PLO—now embracing Fatah and other Palestinian groups—began to operate more and more openly in Jordan despite the government's ban. The monarchy's stock was low after the defeat, and there was public sympathy with the PLO determination to carry the fight to the enemy. PLO raids and the firing of Katyusha rockets into Israel brought such relentless retaliatory shelling from the Israeli army across the Jordan River that the valley on the Jordanian side became almost depopulated as the inhabitants fled to the hills.

More ominously, the PLO created an increasingly powerful presence in Jordan, which it sought to develop as its base of operations against Israel. The popular support it enjoyed, especially in the refugee camps and in the poorer sections of the cities, gave it hospitable bases within the country. The PLO gradually established an authority rivaling the government itself. Fatah, the most powerful faction within the PLO, did not advocate overthrowing the monarchy. But another strong faction, the Popular Front for the Liberation of Palestine (PFLP) led by George Habbash, pursued a doctrine of radical revolution that went beyond the Palestinian cause, and pressed for throwing out the Hashemites.

King Hussein temporized. He was in a difficult spot. By this time, with the 1967 refugee influx, half of his East Bank population was Palestinian. His two powerful neighbors, Syria and Iraq, were strongly supportive of the PLO. A large Iraqi military unit that had been sent to Jordan during the 1967 war had stayed on and was stationed northeast of Amman. Some say that the King had determined as early as 1968 to oust the PLO from Jordan, which he knew his army could do, but because of the sympathy for the Palestinian organization within and outside the country, he waited until its behavior became so outrageous that he would appear justified in acting against it.

Whatever his tactics, it was clear by mid-1970 that the PLO challenge could no longer be ignored. If the King was in fact giving the organization enough rope to hang itself in the public eye, it had begun by then to do so. In July of that year the King and some of his leading officials were ambushed by PLO forces at an Amman street crossing and narrowly escaped death. The army, outraged, attacked PLO units in and near Amman. To force an end to the attacks the PFLP seized fifty-eight foreign hostages in Amman's principal hotel, the Intercontinental, leading to a short-lived cease-fire. The PLO demanded the dismissal of the army commander and other senior military and civilian officials. The King did relieve the commander and one subordinate, which further angered the army. Crisis followed crisis, culminating in a spectacular series of airplane hijackings by the PLO in September that brought three large transports—Swissair, British Overseas Airways and TWA—to an abandoned airstrip in Jordan known as Dawson Field. Though the passengers were eventually released unharmed, the brazen misuse of Jordanian territory by the PLO (the PFLP again) led the army to take to the field in even larger numbers against the guerrillas. The King's intervention was required to prevent more violence. With the army verging on mutiny, the King dismissed his moderate advisers and officials and put the hard-liners in charge. On September 17—"Black September" for the PLO—the army was sent into action against the PLO militias.

When the struggle ended the following July with the final elimination of organized PLO militias in Jordan, Hussein was master in his own house. The regional forces of left-wing pan-Arabism, manipulated for so many years by Nasser, had receded. Nasser himself was dead. The PLO had discovered that Jordan was Jordan, not Palestine. Holding his throne ceased to be an everyday preoccupation for Hussein.

The monarchy has weathered some severe storms. Serious questions about its long-run durability remain, however, that must be examined before the future of the country can be assessed with any assurance. Can a traditional monarchy, however intelligent and conscientious, continue successfully to manage a more and more modern society? To turn the question around: has Jordan evolved into a well-established state, a going concern that will survive and function as a country, whatever forms of government might come and go? Despite the breathing space of recent years, are there political and religious movements that can still threaten the monarchy? Is the Palestinian majority in Jordan destined, one day, to make of the country a Palestinian state?

Modernization and Pressures for Change

The sudden resignation of the Minister of Information in January 1985 revealed that the King's overwhelming influence and style of rule are causing some Jordanians to worry about the future of the country. The Minister is a highly respected woman of Lebanese Druse descent, the widow of one of the country's most admired political leaders, Abdul Hamid Sharaf, who died of a heart attack some years before at the age of forty, while Prime Minister. Her resignation, in protest against the King's policy toward press freedom, exposed this issue to public view in a way that is unusual in Jordan's carefully managed system.

Leila Sharaf was reacting against a letter the King had sent the Prime Minister a few days before, complaining about the failure of the press to support and further his concept of what Jordan should be. "I have noticed," he wrote, "that a number of our newspaper writers have been. . .launching attacks on our social institutions and their customs and values. . . .I have become weary," he continued (expressing a complaint that would be understood in many governments), "of a continued downtrend to frustration of which we see outlines in the newspapers every morning and evening, or in cartoonist drawings which can only cause desperation and lead to loss because these frustrating elements tend to neglect all bright aspects of our life, our national struggle and our Arab heritage." He singled out "writings. . .directed against the tribal life, its norms and traditions." (The precipitant of the King's letter had been controversy in the press, as well as in the upper house of Parliament, over the persistence of tribal law, despite its having been officially abolished by the government in 1976.)[5]

Sharaf, in her response, juxtaposed to the King's formula a principle under which "freedom of expression and the freedom of the press" should be respected "as long as they do not jeopardize the country's security and stability." She saw the need, she said, for an information policy that helped fill the "theological and ideological gap" in the country.

In a subsequent discussion of the issue in her villa on the outskirts of Amman, she expressed the concern often heard in Jordan in one form or another: "We are a nation that has not decided on its identity." She spoke, as Arabs frequently do, in impressionistic and oblique terms, trying to capture a feeling as much as a thought. In referring to a kind of identity crisis in a still-maturing society, she said she sensed in Jordan the total absence of an ideological frame of reference.[6]

---

[5]A revealing postscript to the Sharaf incident was the subsequent appearance, in the February 13 *Jordan Times*, of an article by a well-known Jordanian commentator and former diplomat, headlined "Jordanian bedouins enshrine Arab virtues."

The Sharaf affair did not cut very deeply into the fundamental issues of government. But it did reveal a disquiet with the status quo. How far does the questioning of the current form and style of government go? Does it, above all, show a basic dissatisfaction with the monarchy? Does anyone want a different kind of government?

The short answer to that seems clearly to be "no." It was once the conventional wisdom that monarchy was an outdated political system and that it was just a matter of time before Jordan traded in its government for a later model. Today it is far less clear what other model would be better. Other Middle Eastern experiments have certainly not been encouraging. So you do not find in Jordan today much basic questioning about the desirability of the monarchy.

A Jordanian observer puts it in a nutshell: "A few years ago people still called for a republic. The main fact today is that virtually no one is working to topple the regime." A member of a group preparing itself to become a political party—if parties are again legalized—lists the factors essential for Jordan's future: King, parliamentary system, political parties. A senior political figure, close to the King, says, "as for the King, he has become a necessity for the country—its security blanket and protective umbrella."

The public generally seems to share this view of the King. The East Bankers feel a sense of loyalty to him as *their* King. The Palestinians do not identify with him in the same way. But most appreciate and value his leadership, the stability he gives to what has, perforce, become their country—a country in which the majority of them have done fairly well. The Palestinians in the camps have done less well, needless to say, and are less supportive of the King.

How the public feels about the monarchy as an institution is less clear. The loyalty of bedouin—at one end of Jordan's political scale—tends to be given to the person of the sheikh. The Palestinians, at the other end of the scale, are not especially attracted to the idea of monarchy but are attracted to stability and predictability of government. Many would no doubt say, in addition to appreciating the virtue of the King in this respect, that the monarchy was perhaps the best form of government for Jordan, given the uncertainties of any alternative.

---

[6]Here as elsewhere in this chapter and subsequently, when reference is made to a quote by an individual which is not otherwise cited by reference, it is to a conversation with the author.

It is the nature of the likely alternatives that is perhaps the strongest argument for the monarchy. The two other forms of government that come most readily to people's minds are some type of representative democracy and rule by the military. Concerning the first alternative, a close associate of the King, a businessman and also a thoughtful political observer, argues that Jordan could not function as a parliamentary democracy, as some European states do. "The French have the concept of two kinds of democracy, "he says, "representative and expressive—d'expression. Jordan is the latter kind. People are free to express their wishes, and the governing elite takes them into account. But true representative democracy is not workable here."

Crown Prince Hassan maintains, in his recent book *Search for Peace*, that "Today, everywhere in the Arab East, the experiment with the liberal constitutional system of government appears to have failed. . . .The Western system," he says, "was, in all practical terms, an alien system transferred ready-made not only from another country but from another civilization." He quotes the Middle East scholar Bernard Lewis as calling it "a political order unrelated to the past or present, and profoundly irrelevant to the needs of the future."[7]

Where democratic governmental systems have been tried in the Third World they have often had difficulty achieving legitimacy, and some have developed into highly authoritarian governments, frequently as a result of military coups. The authoritarian governments, military or otherwise, have also found legitimacy elusive and have tended to rule by force. It is possible to envision a similar progression in Jordan, should the monarchy be scrapped for a representative government. The Hashemite monarchy has achieved a fair measure of legitimacy. The government works. Enough stability and order are provided for the society to go about its business, and this is done without unduly repressive measures against the individual citizen. The military establishment is powerful but accepts the right of the King to rule and, with the exception of the 1957 coup attempt, has not tried to enter the political process itself.

All of this, of course, could change. If any major sector of the population should come to feel seriously disadvantaged, if the military should become convinced that they were losing out in a society grow-

---

[7]Hassan ibn Talal, Crown Prince of Jordan, *Search for Peace: The Politics of the Middle Ground in the Middle East* (St. Martin's Press, New York 1984), pp. 45, 51, 52.

ing ever more affluent under their protection or that unacceptable inequities were developing within the civilian society, the general support for the present moderate social contract could break down. The King's legitimacy could erode. The balance is always a fragile one, never established beyond the threat of being overturned. It is this fragility that worries both those who fear any change and those who fear that without change the very conditions may develop that will threaten the system.

These two points of view, these two concerns, are very much alive in Jordan. Some Jordanians question the personalized, one-man show the King runs, however impressive an act it may be. What seems to be involved is a conflict betwen two visions of Jordan: the King's vision of a Jordan that is his to shape and rule; and the vision of an increasingly educated and sophisticated middle class which wants to participate in the management of its own affairs. Put another way, it is a conflict between government by men and government by institutions.

A long-time associate of the King admits that "His Majesty's biggest problem and shortcoming is his vision of the country." But, he adds, "the King's view must be seen in a Middle East context, where he weighs himself against other rulers. He considers himself perhaps the only truly legitimate leader in the Arab world. He has been king for more than thirty years, and his father and grandfather were kings before him. He asks himself 'don't I have as much right to rule as Assad and the others?' With greater popular freedom and representation he knows his powers would be limited. And he believes he can do a better job than the people can, fighting as they would among themselves. As he sees it, they should leave it to him and take care of their own affairs."

King Hussein, this admirer and strong supporter concludes, is "modern, progressive, Western-educated and all the rest of it. But when it comes to Jordan, he sees that in a much more traditional way."

The King rules through two levels of government, if such a formal term can be applied to such an informal and personalized system. The major decisions, especially on foreign affairs and security issues, he makes in a small circle of officials and personal associates. Crown Prince Hassan, his brother and heir apparent, is a member of the circle, as are the two senior Palace officials: the Minister of the Royal Court and the Chief of the Royal Court. The Prime Minister is normally included, certainly one as close to the King as Zeid Rifai, an East Banker who took up the post for the second time in April 1985. So too, the Commander-in-Chief of the armed forces. In addition, there are a number of personal associates and former officials whom the King consults and listens to. Rifai was one of them while he was out of office. Another is Ali Ghandour, a charming and thoughtful sophisticate, a Shia from Lebanon who is head of Alia, the Jordanian airline. These are the King's men, whom he picks not for what they represent but for their personal relationship to him.

For the day-to-day running the country, primarily the domestic affairs, the King relies on the Council of Ministers. This is the formal government cabinet. The King chooses the Prime Minister, looking each time for a man whose outlook and capacities fit the needs of the moment. The position had been filled by a man with a background in the security forces, Ahmad Obeidat, who was said to lack the political sensitivity needed during this period. In the view of many, his replacement by someone like Rifai was overdue in the highly political atmosphere generated by diplomatic moves with the PLO and renewed domestic political life.

What is more important to Hussein's style of rule than the appartus it uses is his personal cultivation of his major constituencies. Jordan is not a big country, and an energetic monarch such as Hussein can touch a lot of bases himself. The tribes are not as central to his control as they once were, but they are still important, and he is sensitive to their concerns. Besides, they reflect his concept of the kind of country Jordan should be. He keeps in touch with the big commercial and banking families—the Tabahs and Mangos, who came decades ago from Syria; the Shomans and Nabulsis, members of prominent West Bank families that spread to the East Bank before World War II. There are Palestinian as well as East Bank families in this group. He provides the Islamic clerical establishment with resources and support, and attempts to co-opt the more militant Islamic organization—the Muslim Brotherhood—with privileges that are the envy of other groups in the country. Above all, perhaps, he cultivates the military forces, with their strong tribal underpinning and traditional loyalty to the institution of the monarchy and the person of the King.

In this way he has been able to maintain a viable balance among competing sectors of the population, in particular between East Bankers and Palestinians. Necessary change has been encouraged—the settlement of the bedouin tribes, for example—but its pace has been kept moderate. No major group has been sufficiently hurt or disadvantaged to turn against the system.

These methods have worked for Hussein. From the East Bank Jordanians, whose origins go back to the tribes, he has won strong personal loyalty and respect. With this group, too, his descent from Fatima, the daughter of the prophet Mohammed, is an important legitimizing factor. His family's continuous reign in Jordan, after the initial annointing by the British, has also contributed. From other major groups, including the Palestinians, he has won respect and confidence.

For all Jordanians, however, the sheer fact of his survival and his success, against such odds, have probably been as important as anything else in giving his rule the legitimacy it obviously enjoys.

It was especially important for him to prove himself during his early years, and he did so. But in a sense he must continue to prove himself if he is to continue to command enough respect to rule effectively. This is especially the case if he tries to go on ruling as he does today, as the father-sheikh-monarch of his people.

Those who assert the need for change cite three reasons: to provide more popular representation; to make the system less fragile in the short run; and to increase the stability of the succession in the longer run.

For some, more democratic representation is an end in itself. A Palestinian whose work keeps him in active circulation says that "in private conversations of both Palestinians and East Bankers this subject always comes up—what is the meaning of life if you do no more than earn and consume and have no role and responsibility in your civic life? Jordan," he exclaims, "is becoming a modern, educated state, but without any political institutions." He argues that "we are pretty lucky in Jordan, with an intelligent and well-intentioned government, but still the people are fed up with just taking orders." This pressure is felt most strongly in their day-to-day life, in the routine contact with government officials about local issues. People make a distinction between the King—a wise but remote figure—and the government, which orders their lives without giving them any say in how they are ordered.

Does the interest in political participation go beyond local issues? In the wake of the 1948 war, it will be recalled, Jordan's new Palestinian citizens pressed for more democracy because they wanted to steer the country back into the fight against Israel. Does some similar aim underlie the democratic agitation today? If it does, it is well hidden. No concerted pressure by Jordan's Palestinian population today on this issue is evident. Moreover, the activity of groups aspiring to become political parties shows that East Bankers seem as anxious as Palestinians to promote democratic political activity.

It is argued by today's activists that the King would be more secure in making policy on all sensitive issues if his decisions were shared by more democratic institutions. They mention, in addition to policy on the Palestinian problem, the handling of the worsening economic situation and the social pressures it could bring. The present system is fragile even over the short run, they argue, because a serious slip by the King or a sudden calamity that he could not control could threaten his credibility and weaken his command over the complex of forces in his country. A possible calamity sometimes mentioned as an example is the destruction by Israeli rightists of the great Jerusalem mosque, the Dome of the Rock, and the wave of violent outrage this would unleash in Jordan and throughout the Islamic world.

In the long run they see an even more serious problem. It is capsulized in a London *Financial Times* article of September 26, 1983, which refers to a "widespread belief in Jordan that [Hussein] will be its last King." This is overstated, but the problem of effective succession is seen as a real one. A leading Jordanian academic says that, barring a calamity or bad mistake, "Hussein should have no trouble holding things together as long as he wants to rule." Even the succession, presumably to Hassan, would probably work. The real problem, he believes, will emerge as Hassan or any other successor tries to imitate the complex, subtle and highly personal method of rule worked out by Hussein. The present King has grown with the country. He has kept in balance the mounting strains as the traditional society has disappeared and a new and more assertive one has taken its place.

A Jordanian who knows the royal family believes that Hussein realizes the system is not so durable. "But we have to live in the short run. Hassan might not be able to do it. He is more rigid than Hussein, who has a good feel for things and is without rigidity. But that is a problem to be faced at the time."

Democratic Institutions and Political Participation

Most Jordanians who press for change seem not to have thought through what precisely the change should be. There appears in the first instance to be a generalized desire for more political participation. The recall of Parliament in 1984 after a ten-year hiatus stimulated public interest in democracy. Its reappearance and the by-elections it necessitated set the political juices running again in the kingdom.

The parliamentary hiatus that came to an end in 1984 had been a response to the designation of the PLO as the sole legitimate representative of the Palestinians by an Arab League Council summit meeting. This move had come in November 1974 at what is commonly referred to as the Rabat summit meeting held in Rabat, Morocco. The King and his government had argued at the time that if the PLO was the representative of the Palestinians, it was no longer appropriate for West Bank Palestinians to have separate, designated representatives in the Jordanian Parliament. The Parliament had been so structured as to give equal representation to the West Bank and East Bank; each had 30 deputies in the lower house.

Another reason to put Parliament on the shelf was the realization after 1967 that any effort to hold general parliamentary elections with the Israelis occupying the West Bank would have tended to formalize the split in the kingdom, since they would have had to be held on the East Bank only. Moreover, holding an election on the East Bank alone was contrary to the constitution. The constitutional problem was subsequently resolved by an amendment providing for general elections to be carried out only on the East Bank, with the newly elected deputies then to choose delegates to represent the West Bank.

The recall of Parliament in 1984 was a political, not a constitutional, act. There were two main reasons for it. First, Hussein was maneuvering to press the PLO to join with Jordan in realistic diplomacy toward a peace settlement with Israel. He saw the value of challenging, in this indirect way, the monopoly over Palestinian representation given the PLO at Rabat, a monopoly that had yielded no real progress toward Palestinian goals. Recalling Parliament, with its West Bank representation, would pose the threat to the PLO that Jordan might once again put itself forward as representing Palestinian interests. Second, the King was being criticized for a lack of democracy in Jordan, and putting Parliament back in business would take some of the pressure off. There was also the technical problem that a quorum was required in a recalled Parliament to complete the new procedures for holding elections. As time went by, the deputies were getting older and dying off, and soon a quorum would be impossible to assemble.

By-elections for the lower house were necessitated by the deaths of twelve deputies—eight from the East Bank, four from the West—since the previous election in 1967. The West Bank representatives were elected by Parliament itself, under the new procedures, but the East Bank elections were full-scale public affairs. True, the security forces prohibited some forms of electioneering, but otherwise the elections were free. Only about half the eligible voters participated (not bad by U.S. standards but low for Jordan), in part because Palestinians felt the elections did not so much concern them. Palestinians still not fully committed to Jordan would not feel much involved in contests primarily among East Bankers for East Bank seats. Islamic-oriented candidates, on the other hand, turned out a high proportion of their more eager constituency to elect three out of the eight deputies.

This renewed political activity has led inevitably to thoughts of more far-reaching democracy. As the October 2, 1984, editorial in the *Jordan Times* put it, "By restoring parliament, our hopes and expectations were not only to discuss laws and by-laws, and allow certain freedoms of speech and expression. Most Jordanians had hoped the step would be the precursor to a real democratic life in the country and a true attempt at popular participation in shaping our political and social life as well." What was the *Times* talking about?

To the extent that there is a focus for the interest in stronger democratic institutions, it is in the legalization of political parties. At the closing session of the lower house of Parliament before the 1984 summer recess, the deputies heard seventeen of their colleagues call for legalizing political parties, lifting of martial law imposed in 1967, and more democratic and constitutional freedoms. This was, it is said, the hottest session of the term. In October 1984 a statement issued by a well-known group of political activists urged Parliament to debate the return of political parties. A *Jordan Times* editorial the following day referred to the "importance of political parties and their inevitable contribution to the democratic process in the Kingdom." A leading parliamentary deputy, an East Banker, echoes this view: "Many people want parties; they want to participate."

In the hope that parties will be legalized, a number of groups are at work preparing themselves to set up business when the time arrives. This is not done *sub rosa*. Government officials, businessmen, prominent professionals, even a few cabinet members form the core of these nascent political organizations. Meetings are held openly.

The most active of the groups is an interesting mix. It calls itself the Unionist Democratic Association. At its head is a medical doctor, Jamal Shair, owner of the Ahli Hospital in Amman. An East Banker and a Muslim, he was at one time Minister of Rural and Municipal Affairs. The medical director of the same hospital, Dr. Carlos Dimas, a Christian Palestinian from the Christian town of Beit Jallah near Jerusalem, is also a member. There are engineers, economists, lawyers, both East Bankers and Palestinians.

Shair's group is the only one with a program spelled out in writing. Shair himself is a former Baathist, and the idea of Arab unity strongly flavors the group's platform. The first line of its first principle states: "The Jordanian people are part of the Arab nation." The platform goes on to speak of the unity of both banks of the Jordan, the need for Arab unity to help the Arabs "come out of the present state of fragmentation, weakness and backwardness," the importance of democracy, and the need for overall planning in the economic and social spheres to preserve the balance between the public and private sectors and secure economic growth and social justice. The struggle between the superpowers endangers peace, the platform maintains, and Jordan must reject any involvement by strengthening Arab solidarity with the nonaligned countries.

Among the other groups, the strongest is the Arab Constitutionist Party, with what it calls liaison houses in towns and villages of the country. It is headed by the Interior Minister of a previous cabinet, Suleiman Afar, and four other former cabinet ministers are among its members. It is considered a party of the Establishment and generally reflects government views and the status quo. Jordanian security is a major concern together with the preservation of a dominant position for East Bankers.

The Jordan National Party is heavily East Banker as well, though its strength comes mainly from Amman. The Constitutional Front has followers among the tribal leaders, but it is thought to have even less political strength than the others. The fifth group, the National Democratic Party, has recently lost momentum, and an offshoot has formed under the leadership, *inter alia*, of two former Interior Ministers with tribal backgrounds.

The nascent parties, despite the presence in their leadership of former cabinet ministers, are not thought to have much political weight. They have not yet aroused broad public interest and draw their membership from a rather thin layer of politically-interested activists. This may show that the public does not really care about more political participation, as some Jordanian observers claim, or that these particular groups are unexciting. Both answers probably have some truth.

Whatever may be their shortcomings, these groups are not the abstract, intellectual parties that often develop in societies with little political life. They do have their intellectual debates, but at the same time they show the sort of pragmatism that seems especially typical of Jordan. At this stage they are said to want as members people with sufficient influence and safe political coloration to help get them legalized. When the members of one group were asked about the issues that future elections would be fought around, if parties were permitted to run, they listed a number of fairly obvious ones: religious-secular, rich-poor, tribal-nontribal, Palestinian-East Banker. But they then turned to what they obviously saw as the real meat of politics—the organization of well-balanced slates of candidates.

"We would need to have an important tribal candidate in each part of the country," they said. "About 20 percent will vote just for tribal association." For the eight seats in Amman they would want four Arab Muslims, two Christians, and two Circassians (Muslims who migrated from Russia to the area in the nineteenth century). As to their political opinions, the candidates should have "generally liberal views." More important, they should have political weight personally and be members of important families.

The restoration of parties is not a step the King and the current cabinet will take lightly, however. The experience of the 1950s and 1960s is still recent and still bitter. True, the political groups of today are taking great pains to demonstrate their loyalty. Their leaders and other political observers assert that there is a different political environment now in which the troublesome movements of those years—Baathism, Communism, Nasserism—have been largely discredited. Jordan, they say, has jelled politically and is no longer so vulnerable to regional winds of change.

That Jordan is a different country today is conceded by even the most conservative leadership. One such adviser to the King worries nevertheless that there are still too many foreign "lines" flowing through the kingdom. He is distressed that freedom of speech exercised in the recalled Parliament sometimes seems irresponsible. "Parliamentary immunity does not mean you can say whatever you think," he exclaims. One finds people overlooking "their basic duty as deputies," he says; parties would only stimulate such tendencies, by which particular interests are put before those of the country.

One of the top men in the government points out, in addition, that even when there are parties, most of the candidates run as independents. He sees no reason why the next election should not be contested by independents without the need for parties.

The issue, for the time being, is moot in any case. There can be no election while the King and his advisers are pursuing a strategy looking toward eventual peace negotiations over the Palestinian question. The holding of elections would immediately raise the whole delicate question of Jordan's relationship with the Palestinian people and with the West Bank in particular. The very election process, choosing a House of Deputies half representing the East Bank and half the West Bank, would throw the issue into sharp relief. The peace diplomacy and the questions it raises—like this one—would in addition be made central issues in the campaign. The relationship between the government and the PLO is a fragile one. No one in the government wants to see this delicate boat rocked by unneccesary domestic waves; the international turbulence is enough.

A senior palace official puts it this way: "The next election depends on when and whether the West Bank can vote. We cannot have an election now."

Whatever the threat these pressures for more democracy may pose for the stability of the monarchy, they come basically from supporters of the King and the present system. There are other threats, some that are less benign.

One is the kind of subversive operation that is run from outside Jordan and carried out in the main by professionals. Less serious but a continuing source of low-level pressure are the opposition groups, nominally domestic but reflecting foreign goals and ideologies and backed from abroad. Some openly aim at the destruction of the monarchy, others want to embarrass its policies and redirect its alignments. Finally, there are larger segments of the population that are breeding grounds of dissent—primarily the refugee camps and the university students—and one large group that poses a problem difficult to measure but potentially serious—the Islamic "movement."

Foreign-run subversion has long been a problem for Jordan. A small country surrounded across long borders by powerful neighbors, it has a history of that most familiar and most worrying action, the political assassination. With the present line-up of forces and policies in the Middle East, these operations tend to have a Syrian label. The assassination of the moderate PLO Executive Committee member, Fahd Kawasmeh, in early 1985, was a classic Syrian-backed action. At another time, Iraq or Egypt was and might be again the main threat in the kaleidescopic world of Middle East politics.

Successful attacks on Jordanian interests usually take place in third countries, primarily assassinations of Jordanian officials and diplomats. This is testimony to the alertness of Jordanian security at home, where virtually all such operations are detected and blocked.

Hard-line opposition within the country comes mainly from the Jordanian Communist Party, the Jordanian Baath Party, and the rejectionist, anti-Hashemite factions of the PLO. There is the familiar proliferation of left-wing groups, some composed of and supported by the Communists and Baathists: the Committee for the Defense of Democratic Freedoms, the National Democratic Grouping, the Jordanian Peoples Revolutionary Party, Popular Organization Committees in Jordan, and the Jordanian Peoples Government. These groups oppose Jordan's association with the West, the United States in particular, and call for cooperation with leftist regimes in Syria and elsewhere in the Arab world. Some oppose the Jordanian monarchy as such.

The groups are outlawed in Jordan. Under tight security pressure their active cadres are small and conduct only a limited, clandestine existence. Even so they can be dangerous. The Jordanian Peoples Revolutionary Party, an offshoot of the Baath Party, has conducted small-scale bomb attacks against Americans in Jordan, for example, which failed to cause casualties but not for want of trying.

University students, in Jordan as elsewhere, and the Palestine refugees living jammed together in crowded camps are groups in which dissent flourishes more easily than elsewhere in Jordanian society. Neither is a serious problem today, but if present restrictions on political organizing, demonstrations and gatherings were significantly relaxed, it is likely that political activity would develop here, some of which would be hostile to the regime and its policies. One Palestinian whose work brings him in contact with camp refugees comments that if the tight security grip were loosened, an upsurge of troublesome activity would follow, though the problem is much reduced in periods, such as 1985, when the regime and the PLO were on better terms.

One group of students is of special concern to security authorities. Some 60,000 Jordanians are studying in foreign universities, some of them in Eastern Europe, others in Marxist South Yemen. The activities of students, especially those studying in Communist countries, are carefully watched by security personnel. They are considered to be more exposed to radical and anti-monarchical philosophies while they are abroad. The government has been promoting, with some opposition from the public and Parliament, a law that would require all applications for passport renewal to be reviewed by the Interior Ministry as an extra security screening opportunity. Students are the main target.

Islam and the Fundamentalist Movement

The Islamic phenomenon is in a class by itself. It draws its inspiration and strength from sources deep in Arab culture. Islam has been the prescribed and generally accepted way of life for Arabs for centuries. Its precepts, though they can be and often are ignored in practice, cannot be openly contested in the Islamic world, and they have a legitimacy that makes them a powerful basis for action. At the same time, Islam is deeply political, in the Western sense of the term, because it prescribes the proper conduct for all aspects of life. It is the source of law and the guide to collective behavior of society, for governors and governed alike.

Crown Prince Hassan writes in his *Search for Peace* that "In the building of a nation, the purpose of Islam is not simply to exhort the faithful to do good and avoid evil, but to construct a perfect and righteous society—a community in which the Divine Laws of God will prevail. Islam, as such, knows no distinction between a religious and a secular realm."[8]

For decades the Muslim world has been going through a secularizing process. The process is familiar to Westerners because Christian society has been going through it for a much longer period. There is, however, one important distinction between the two experiences. To an Arab Muslim, secularization means Westernization, a perception with much truth. Most of what is "modern" and secular about present-day Islamic societies has come from the West, including the concept of Arab nationalism itself.

Secularization has been accelerating in the Arab world just at a time when many Arabs have felt an especially strong sense of frustration and failure as a people. Inability of the Arabs to prevent the establishment of Israel in particular and their continuing humiliation at the hands of the Israelis, whom they see as a Western intrusion into the Arab world, have been the most important cause of this despair.

Inevitably a backlash against Western secularization has come. Return to the purity of Islam is seen by many as the only way to overcome the weakness, failure and factionalism that have beset the Arabs. It is by no means only "political," however. As in the West, the highly secular life is found personally unfulfilling by many, and a return to religion seems the answer.

By any standard, Jordanian society is secular and Westernized. The monarchy itself was established by a Western government along the lines of Western models. Yet a strong conservative tradition has kept Jordan in the middle ground between such states as Syria, with political institutions and philosophies that have an anti-religious cast,

---

[8]*Op. cit.* p. 40.

and Saudi Arabia, which tries to live by Islamic precepts. The Hashemite lineage back through the daughter of the Prophet may not qualify the King as a devout Muslim in the eyes of the most faithful, but it makes it harder to attack him as an enemy of Islam.

The Jordanian government has, in addition, actively promoted Islam. The Ministry of Education came under the control of Islamic enthusiasts in the early 1960s, and a strong religious program in the schools has resulted. The Ministry of Islamic Affairs and Holy Places is said to subsidize the wearing of religious dress by Jordanian women, paying them with funds donated by well-to-do families with strong Islamic interests.

Islamic activism in Jordan today falls into two broad categories. Some organizations, either political or religious, have been around for some decades; and there is also the new, largely unorganized Islamic fervor that has arrived on the scene in Jordan as in other countries of the Middle East. The line between them is not clear and hard, but it is there.

The Muslim Brotherhood is the most important of the older political-religious organizations. Founded in Egypt in 1928, it made its appearance in the West Bank in 1946. Eventually it became widespread on both Banks. The Brotherhood believes in using political action to establish a pure Islamic society, including, of course, its government. This group has been banned in some Arab countries, but the Jordanian leadership has always supported it with funds, facilities and, most important, permission to operate in an almost semi-official capacity. In return, the Brothers supported the monarchy during its trials in the 1950s and have not pursued the subversive course that has made them such a problem in Egypt and Syria.

The membership of the Brotherhood numbers in the many thousands. It enjoys a strong influence over the mosques and in the Ministry of Islamic Affairs and Holy Places and the Ministry of Education.

The smaller, more radical Tahrir (liberation) Party is banned but operates clandestinely in a limited way. Like the Brotherhood, it aims at establishing an Islamic society. Unlike the Brotherhood, though, it explicity calls for the destruction of existing states as a prerequisite.

These groups are familiar fixtures. What engages the attention and evokes the concern of Jordanians today is the appearance of an amorphous but very real movement back to Islam by many people from all levels of society.

Evidence of it is everywhere. At Amman University it seems that half at least of the young women wear an adaptation of the traditional veil—not over the face, but a white scarf around the head worn with a a long native dress. Many women in the street are similarly dressed.

The mosques on Friday, the Islamic holy day, are especially impressive. Everyone agrees that fifteen years ago the attendance was thin and largely well along in years. Not so today. On a Friday in mid-1985 at midday prayers, the crowd overflowed the spacious precincts of the central Hussein Mosque in downtown Amman. Inside, the mosque was jammed. Crowds filled the outer courtyard. More worshippers spilled out onto the sidewalk and into the street. Sheets of blue plastic were brought for them to kneel on in the road while traffic made its way around them. The faithful filled the sidewalk on down the street in front of the shops adjacent to the Mosque for a block or more. About half wore the long, traditional robe. More than half seemed relatively young. On a nearby side street a little corner mosque presented the same scene. A young man in long robe and glasses ran out of a cross-street, straw prayer mat under his arm, late for prayers.

The director of a large camp for Palestinian refugees near Amman claims that Islamic observance in the camps is even stronger than in the country as a whole. This has been especially true in the last two to three years, he says, with the camp's eleven mosques (for a population of 65,000) more crowded than at any other time. More young people are now involved.

The three deputies elected to the Parliament in the by-election of 1984 as Islamic candidates have joined with three or four others of similar persuasion to form a bloc that has on occasion been troublesome. It has raised issues not necessarily widely popular but issues no Muslim can contest, such as banning alcholic beverages in the kingdom. (Remarks one Deputy, not of their number, "If they go too far, the government will twist their ears.")

Radio and television time devoted to religion has increased. Ramadan[9] fasting is more strictly observed than it once was.

No one knows what to make of this new Islamic manifestation or how to measure it, in Jordan or elsewhere in the Arab world for that matter. It seems not to be an organized movement (though the term "movement" is frequently used for it in the loose sense), but how is it to be otherwise explained?

A thoughtful commentary by one of the newly elected Islamic parliamentary deputies sheds some light. The upsurge of interest in

---

[9]Ramadan is a month of fasting to commemorate the revelation to Mohammed of the first verses of the Koran, the Islamic holy book.

Islam must be seen against the backdrop of recent history, he begins. The mistrust of Islam was sown in the Middle East by the West in the late nineteenth century. The Arabs were given ideas such as pan-Arabism and nationalism—in themselves colonial ideas. Nationalism is a secular concept, opposed to Islam.

His father and grandfather, he continues, like other educated men of the time, were nationalists. He himself began as a nationalist "programmed to oppose my religion." In doing university research on Islam in 1967, however, he found his identity. He asked himself, "What are you doing? You are playing around, but your country needs you."

He was one of very few at that time, he recalls. Now there are many more, but it is not a movement. The adherents of the new Islamic wave are "self-motivated." He feels, partly for this reason, that the trend to Islam falls short. Islam is a demanding faith. It requires study before one becomes involved, but this is not happening. Islam is not a philosophy. Philosophies cost nothing, but religion makes demands on the faithful, requires changes in their lives. Islam in particular requires changes not just of the individual but of society. This man's generation was, however, brought up on individualism; and coherent organized change is not occurring. Only a major disaster of some sort could galvanize such change, he concludes.

He is gloomy about the prospects. Jordan will not become Islamic, he predicts. He seems to be saying that many of the people who profess the new Islamic fervor are not serious about it but are looking for an easy solution to individual needs. He seems also to say that Jordanian society cannot be changed without the leadership, program and organization this Islmaic revival does not have. It cannot be done individually and by increments.

Not that the movement is totally without structure. There are groups organized around local charismatic figures, but they seem to have little connection with one another. Prosyletization is also said to be occurring in an organized way within the armed forces, which worries the government. Some of the top people in the Islamic chaplaincy are fundamentalists.

Estimates differ as to the strength of the revival. A former Information Minister believes that without more political education of Jordanians they will become "captives of the Islamic movement." She also believes that if the Palestinian problem is not solved, the movement will grow. The by-election campaigns of Islamic candidates did indeed stress this connection with such slogans as: "No solution to the Palestinian question except through Islam," and "No to Camp David and no to Reagan. Elect Dr. Kufchi who believes that Islam. . .is the sole road to Palestine." Verses from the Koran were used in warning against deviation from the Islamic faith and asserting that the occupied lands would never by restored without a return to pure Islam. Fundamentalists also tend to be more uncompromising than Jordanians generally on the question of peace, insisting that all of Palestine must be returned to Islam.

Other Jordanians see the movement as having peaked. A leading academic argues that since it has not made headway among intellectuals or upwardly mobile elites, it is failing. Some say the impetus for its growth came from the Iranian revolution, and that the excesses of that revolution have discouraged believers and caused the tide to ebb.

Another well-known scholar offers what is perhaps the most widespread view. "No visible domestic source of trouble seems likely to produce a serious threat to the stability of the monarchy except possibly the Islamic movement," he says. "And that is worrying because it is such an unknown. Some failure or mistake or weakness on the part of the regime could trigger it."

What is most unnerving about the movement, in fact, is the impression it gives of waiting in the wings for something to happen, for the present system to fail, perhaps, or for a leader to emerge to galvanize it. Without that it remains a large, inchoate populist phenomenon with an unmeasurable but worrying potential.

The Security Grip

In the face of these threats and potential threats, Jordanian security forces retain a tight grip. At the same time, the life of the average Jordanian is relatively free of security controls. This balance is achieved by focusing security efforts on what are thought to be the danger areas, avoiding the sort of broad regime that keeps tight control on everyone. Another way of putting it is that security is as tight as it needs to be, and the great majority of the public does not have to be controlled.

Three government services have security roles: the Army, the police and the General Intelligence Directorate (GID). Main reliance is on the GID, generally referred to in Jordan as the Mukhabarat—meaning intelligence.

The GID is a civilian organization with somewhat the same mix of functions as the FBI in the United States—intelligence, counterintelligence, police work, and enforcement. It operates out of a large building complex in the business section of the city. It is a relatively large service and is given high marks for effectiveness by Jordanians and Americans familiar with its activities. It is, like the army, dominated by East Bank Jordanians. The Jordanian public seems to regard it with respect tinged with fear. It has no doubt played roughly with some opponents over the years. Stories abound that attribute to it a ubiquitous presence and harsh methods, including the use of torture in investigations. In today's Jordan, according to outsiders acquainted with its work, it does not have the represssive character or the most brutal methods associated with security police in more dictatorial regimes. As to ubiquitousness, it does not seem to miss a great deal, but neither is it much in evidence.

A Jordanian professional woman remembers when security was much more intrusive. She returned to Amman in 1973, after a long absence abroad. She recalls that in those days one could walk down the street at noon and have one's passport checked; driving in the city one could be stopped and have one's car searched. Today, she notes, this is virtually unheard of.

Jordanians can drive anywhere in the country as freely as one can in the United States, except for a few sensitive border areas—near the Syrian border, near the port of Aqaba, or in the Jordan valley. There one encounters checkpoints, but nowhere else. There is no system whereby one must register with the police in the neighborhood where he lives. A Jordanian can move from one place to another without telling anyone in authority.

A pattern of identity documents does, however, give the government a good picture of the population and considerable leverage where it counts. There is no requirement that everyone carry an identity card; but everyone over the age of 16 has one, and most carry it. Heads of families are issued a "family card" by the Ministry of Interior listing family members. This and the identity card must be produced to obtain a passport.

The main security control is the passport. Not just a travel document, as in the United States, it is needed to get a job. The GID must authorize its issuance. If you are in their black books you may not get one. Beyond that, to study abroad or work for the government you need a certificate of good conduct, which the GID issues.

A Palestinian, who might well himself be a subject of GID interest, tells about his son's passport problems. The young man attended school for a period in a Communist country. He finished and came back to Jordan, intending to go abroad again for another course of study. The GID, the father says, held his passport because of his earlier stay abroad and told him he could get it back only by working for them as an informant. He refused and is now unable to leave the country.

This man's son, of course, falls into one of the categories that get special security attention. Refugee camps are another target of attention. There is said to be a GID office in each camp. The director of one camp says he is not allowed to show visitors around the camp without GID permission, and the security man usually comes along when permission is given.

The tight security grip extends to public political activity, and this is an area where it affects the general population more broadly. Public demonstrations, even those that support a cause favored by the government, are seldom permitted. In August 1982 a group of women attempted to march on the American Embassy to present a petition against what was seen as American support for the Israeli invasion of Lebanon, but they were stopped by the police. Only after the massacres in the Sabra and Shatila refugee camps in Beirut was a demonstration permitted, this time by a group representing the professional associations in Jordan. Mass meetings, public rallies, loudspeakers and posters in the streets were prohibited during the 1984 parliamentary elections. The concern seems to be that even a benign demonstration could get out of hand, be misused by less benign elements. One Jordanian was led to exclaim that it was easier to have a demonstration on the West Bank, under the Israelis, than in Jordan.

The mosques are not exempt. Sermons delivered at Friday prayers are screened by the Ministry of Islamic Affairs and Holy Places. Such control has been exercised at other times in Jordan's history, but this particular requirement stems from the early days of the Iranian revolution. The GID, in addition—and more to the point—keeps a close eye on mosque activities, including the sermons, to deal with religion that goes over the line into subversion.

The press is controlled by a form of self-censorship. As the editor of one of the leading dailies explains it: "We have a press free of censorship and intervention, but there is self-censorship. We hear [from the authorities] about our exceeding the limits by telephone calls and meetings." Referring to the King's letter "to placate the tribes" that had criticized the press for the way it exercised its freedom, he remarked that it had not been followed up by any actual measures. "We aspire to a free press," he concluded, "but we recognize that these are difficult times for the country."

Outsiders and some Jordanians inevitably question whether the security restrictions on political organizations and public political activity are necessary. Security people, of course, do not want to wait to learn the answer to a question like that; they take no chances. The margin for error in Jordan is less than in many other countries. Frustrations at home, among Palestinians especially but by no means exclusively, coupled with pressure from powerful neighbors who have some capacity to exploit those frustrations, make for a worrisome unpredictability. A better-be-safe-than-sorry attitude is natural. Even some Jordanians who wish for more political freedom wonder whether it would be safe. The professional woman quoted earlier about less intrusive security goes on to say that she does not know whether freer politics would be "constructive." The Muslim Brotherhood might become more powerful.

In looking back on the questions this chapter set out to examine, what conclusions do the intervening pages suggest?

Jordan is very much King Hussein's country. He has shaped it and he rules it. There seems little disposition on the part of Jordanians, including Palestinians, to replace his monarchy with another form of government, and there are important groups and institutions determined to prevent any such replacement.

The fundamental strength of the monarchy lies in the social contract that provides a good deal of satisfaction to the principal sectors of the population. The King is permitted to rule, and the country is given security and order and a relatively high degree of personal freedom for the individual citizen.

It does not necessarily follow that the King is essential to the existence of Jordan as a state. It seems likely, though, that a Jordan without a monarchy that functioned as the monarchy does under Hussein would have difficulty in today's circumstances maintaining the present balance among population groups and institutions and between stability and individual freedom, as well as the present relatively efficient economic system.

King Hussein can very likely stay on top of events as long as he lives and wants to rule. His one-man, paternalistic style is inherently fragile, but he is good at it. Doubts about the durability of the monarchy arise mainly over the succession. With the security lid still on and the army still loyal to the monarchy, an orderly succession can probably be achieved. Whether a new king could then make Hussein's methods work for him is an open question.

Long-term durability might be enhanced by developing a more institutionalized government, patterned, for example, on European constitutional monarchies. Trying to remodel the ship of state in today's heavy seas would have costs in short-term stability. In any case, this King is not going to give up enough power to give life to more representative institutions. And it is possible that European models are not appropriate for Jordan. The present system may actually be the best system, with whatever weaknesses it has. No system is without weaknesses.

The desire for greater participation in government is real, but it does not seem likely to destabilize the monarchy if it is not satisfied. It is to some degree offset by concerns that more political freedom will give opportunity to the wrong elements. The public wants more say mainly about day-to-day domestic affairs, not foreign or security policy. If the recalled Parliament and the government work together, they can give some satisfaction to this desire without raising broader issues that affect stability. Meanwhile, democracy does exist at lower and more local levels—in the selection of municipal councils, and the governing boards of cooperatives and professional associations.

The most serious threat to the monarchy and the country is the possibility of an unexpected event that jars the body politic profoundly. The more unsettling candidates for such a role involve the Palestinian problem. The one danger most often mentioned by Jordanians is that such an event could galvanize the Islamic movement into concerted action. As of now, the Islamic revival phenomenon seems relatively passive, without organization, leadership or program. It is nevertheless an unknown of conceivably great potential power.

The tight but not broadly intrusive security regime, prudent in the circumstances, seems likely to be able to hold the center against the most evident threats. In the Middle East, of course, the unexpected must be expected, and therein lies whatever question mark hangs over the head of the monarchy.

3

Jordanian Society: Cohesion or Conflict?

F or some sixty-five years the Hashemites have been trying to weld diverse groups of people into a single nation loyal to their rule. They started with territory that had no historical coherence as an entity and people with primarily local or tribal loyalties, and it has been an uphill struggle. For much of the period the state as a focus of identity has tended to be lost between purely local and broader pan-Arab loyalties. Groups that transferred their allegiance from the local have often fixed on the King rather than the state as the object of loyalty. Above all, the dramatic influx of Palestinians led to the existence of two societies side by side. A real question arose as to whether the Palestinians would be "Jordanianized," or whether the old Jordanian society would be "Palestinianized." Or would a new society develop, a blend of the two?

The life expectancy of the monarchy, and indeed of the country as we know it today, depends in part on how these processes are working themselves out.

The Suspect Seam

The most suspect seam in Jordanian society is that which binds Palestinian-Jordanians to East Bank Jordanians—a seam especially vulnerable to the kind of external pressure that appears most likely to threaten the cohesion of the state.

Palestinians make up a little more than half the population of Jordan today. Figures are inexact, and there is no official statistical breakdown of the population by Palestinian and East Banker origins. Government statistics for 1983 show a total population of about 2.5 million. This does not include Jordanians, mainly of Palestinian origin, who had lived longer than the preceding year in the Persian Gulf states or elsewhere outside Jordan, a number estimated at several hundred thousand.

Of this 2.5 million total, the commonly accepted guess is that Palestinians number somewhat more than 1.3 million. Roughly 200,000 of these live in refugee camps provided by the government, where they receive health, education and other services from UNRWA (United Nations Relief and Works Agency), the U.N. agency for Palestinian refugees.

This is not the only seam in the society. It is not the only source of strain. But it is different in two ways from other divisions. First, the Palestinians outnumber the original East Bank Jordanians; and second, the Palestinians did not come to the country, as most other immigrants have, with the intention of settling in and making their homes there.

The East Bankers, seen today as the "indigenous" population of Jordan, are themselves a mixture of long-time inhabitants and immigrants who have arrived within the seven decades since World War I. Perhaps 300,000 people lived in the country in 1920, nearly half of them nomads, the rest townspeople, villagers and semi-nomads. Nomadic tribes moved in and out of the area with the seasons.

Before and after World War I there was continuing movement back and forth between the east and west banks of the Jordan River. The river is an arbitrary boundary that even after the establishment of Transjordan remained highly permeable. Some leading families had long exercised influence over areas that spanned the river. Traditionally close ties existed between certain cities on the two sides: Salt in Jordan and Nablus on the West Bank, for example, or Kerak and Hebron. An active smuggling traffic and other forms of trade were carried on under arrangements between leading trading families on both banks. Some Palestinian families had established themselves in East Bank towns long before 1948, one of them being the Tuqans, the family of Hussein's third wife, Queen Alia.

The first modern immigrants were probably the Syrians, who fled south after the French chased Feisal out of Damascus. This Syrian influx continued into the 1920s. The next identifiable group was the Hashemites themselves, Abdallah and the few hundred tribesmen he brought north with him from the Hejaz. In succeeding years Jordan remained a haven for people seeking refuge from turmoil elsewhere in the region. By 1946, on the eve of the great Palestinian wave, the population had grown to about 434,000.

The Rifai family, from which have come two of Jordan's Prime Ministers, is a revealing example of the freedom of movement in the region until recent years and the arbitrariness of the present boundaries. The grandfather of Zeid Rifai was born in Southern Syria in the days of Ottoman rule. He became an administrator in the service of the Empire, serving here and there, wherever his assignments took him. His son Samir, Zeid Rifai's father, was born when the grandfather was serving in Safed, in Palestine, now Sfat in Israel. Samir Rifai began his career as a civil servant of another empire under the British Mandate. As such he was seconded to help establish the civil service of the Emirate of Transjordan, coming to Amman in the early 1920s. When his second term expired in 1935, he stayed on in the service of the Hashemites, becoming Prime Minister in the early post-World War II years. He and his son, Zeid, though of Syrian and then Palestinian origin, are considered deep-dyed East Bankers in the spectrum of Jordanian society today.

The cut-off date for Palestinians was 1948. Those who came to Jordan in that year or subsequently remained "Palestinians," even though they were accepted into Jordanian society and given Jordanian citizenship. This was not an arbitrary decision of the Jordanians. It accurately reflected the totally different circumstances under which these Palestinians arrived. It reflected as well the state of mind they brought with them. Whether they fled to the West Bank and Jordan to escape the fighting or to avoid living under Israeli rule, or were forcibly driven out by the Israelis, all left unwillingly. They arrived embittered at their loss and determined to go back eventually.

Palestinians fled to Jordan from a society that was in many ways more highly developed than that on the East Bank. This was especially true at the early stage, in 1948, when Jordan was largely a rural country of small towns and villages. Up to that time, especially during the 1920s and 1930s, the East Bank (then the Emirate of Transjordan) had been remote from world affairs and outside influences—seen in retrospect by some as having been an idyll.

The Palestinians came from quite a different experience. Many had led urban lives in the cities of Jaffa and Jerusalem, or in the complex of large towns in between. They were, on the average, better educated and more sophisticated. And far from having led a cloistered existence, they had lived for two decades under the impact of the Zionist influx and the Arab struggle against it. In the process they had developed a higher degree of political awareness and had become more conscious than the Jordanians of their political identity.

The relationship between the East Bank Jordanians and the mass of unwilling refugees was inevitably difficult. It was vastly complicated, too, by the sudden expansion of the state at the same time to embrace the West Bank with its indigenous Palestinian population and its own hordes of refugees. Years of turmoil ensued. The refugees resisted integration into Jordanian society, and the government, while pursuing enlightened integration policies, ruthlessly suppressed their efforts to continue the struggle with Israel.

From the outset, though, there were important differences among the Palestinians in their adaptation to the new circumstances. The notable families that supported Abdallah were well rewarded with economic and political power. Some major West Bank families expanded their lucrative economic enterprises to the East Bank. Some formed links with leading East Bank families to dominate certain areas of trade or commerce. For these Palestinians the post-1948 years brought economic prosperity.

Other prominent Palestinian families that had opposed the Hashemites did not fare so well. They watched their dominance of Palestinian society and their economic privileges slip away. It was this group that did much to inspire and lead the revolt against the King's rule in the mid-1950s.

The much more numerous middle- and lower-middle-class Palestinians who came to East Bank Jordan—professionals, intellectuals, merchants, tradesmen—were caught in the whipsaw of conflicting reactions to their situation but generally set about establishing themselves economically. More enterprising and better equipped with education and skills than the local society, they eventually became dominant in the professions and all kinds of business: banking, insurance, manufacturing, construction, shipping, food processing, trade and commerce of various kinds. They concentrated in the cities, especially Amman, where they now constitute 75 percent of the population. Meeting an East Banker in Amman seems at times as rare as meeting a native Californian in Los Angeles.

Those refugees without resources or skills that could be used in their new situation remained apart from Jordanian society and economy. The great majority went into refugee camps because they could not otherwise survive. These people, together with the notable families of the opposition, continued to be the most alienated from the regime.

Some homogenization took place after the first few difficult years. Some important differences between the Palestinians and the East Bankers diminished or disappeared. The government made every effort to incorporate the Palestinians into the society and, to the extent that distinctions between the two groups remained, to balance the interests of both, for example, by giving Palestinians an equal share of cabinet posts. With rapid improvement in public education and experience in the developing economic infrastructure, the learning and skill levels of the East Bankers rose to match that of the Palestinians. A prominent banker comments that his bank, founded by Palestinians in the 1930s, had to be staffed until well after 1948 with West Bankers. By 1985, it was relying on a staff that was predominantly East Banker. The inferiority complex of the original Jordanian population gradually faded.

The melting pot was beginning to work when the establishement of the PLO in 1964 and the Arab-Israeli war in 1967 set in motion a train of events that reversed the process.

The founding of the PLO gave new life to the idea of a separate Palestinian national identity. The process accelerated after 1967 as the PLO, dismayed by the failure of the Arab armies in the Six Day War, took the struggle more into its own hands. Palestinian organizations such as the Palestinian Red Crescent Society—the Islamic equivalent of the Red Cross—were established, giving added tangibility to a separate Palestinian nationality.

The effects for Jordan were compounded by the wave of new refugees who fled to Jordan after the 1967 war from the West Bank and the Gaza Strip. Eighty-five percent of these Palestinians came from the West Bank, a part of Jordan since 1948. The homogenizing process at work between Palestinians and East Bankers in East Bank Jordan between 1948 and 1967 had had little effect on Palestinians in the West Bank, however. If anything, the latter had grown increasingly disenchanted with Jordan under what most of them considered to be Jordanian occupation. Thus refugees arrived on the East Bank in 1967 with strong feelings of Palestinian nationalism and little interest in becoming Jordanian.

During 1969 and 1970 the PLO set up a virtually autonomous administration within Jordan, leading to the bloody fighting of 1970–71 between the Jordanian army and the PLO militias. While the "Black September" conflict was fought between the army and the militias, not between Jordanians and Palestinians, it nevertheless had far-reaching implications for Jordanian society. It was, as a former cabinet minister describes it, "a clash of nationalisms, the first crack in Jordanian society." Although Jordan's Palestinian population kept their heads down and avoided taking sides, the estrangement of the PLO and the Jordanian state that followed the conflict increased the sense of separation between Palestinians and East Bank Jordanians. East Bankers inclined to be suspicious of Palestinians became more so, although the government tried to keep clear the distinction between the PLO and the Palestinian population of the country.

The major test came in 1974. The Arab League's designation of the PLO as the sole legitimate representative of the Palestinian people—including, presumably, those living in Jordan as Jordanian citizens—put in question the whole relationship between Jordan and the Palestinians. The carefully nurtured ambiguities that had made it possible for the Jordanian state and society to work seemed threatened. Many Jordanian-Palestinians were unhappy with the decision for this reason.

A strong reaction followed in East Bank circles. A senior official in the government of the time recalls that "some East Bank Jordanians were so angry that they even wanted to remove Jordanian citizenship from the Palestinians and call new elections in the East Bank alone." The King and Prime Minister Rifai opposed extreme measures, realizing that these could tear the country apart. But they recognized the necessity of adopting policies that seemed responsive to the change decreed by the Rabat decision, and they were sensitive to the political need for actions that were responsive to the sharp reaction of East Bank Jordanians.

A period followed in which there was talk of Jordanizing Jordan, of putting Jordan's own East Bank house in order, Jordan for the Jordanians, and the like. There were proposals to put an end to the dual identity of the Palestinians, to oblige them to choose—Jordan, love it or leave it, in effect. Jordanian financial subsidies to West Bank communities and institutions, which had been continued to some extent since 1967, were stopped. They were picked up in part in 1978 by a joint PLO-Jordanian committee set up to channel to the West Bank funds from other Arab states. The governments of a number of Gulf countries had pledged amounts for this purpose at an Arab League Council summit meeting in Baghdad in 1978.

The government that replaced Rifai's in 1976, under East Banker Mudar Badran, was more vigorous in promoting a Jordanian-first point of view than Rifai had been. It went so far as to propose cutting off the salaries of Jordanian civil servants on the West Bank—primarily teachers—that Amman was paying even under the Israeli occupation. These, too, would have been taken over by the PLO-Jordanian committee using non-Jordanian funds, when they were available. A leading Jordanian loyalist on the West Bank protested that these salaries were a Jordanian obligation, and the idea was abandoned.

The proportion of Palestinians in the cabinet was dropped from a half to a quarter. Some Palestinian government personnel were let go and replaced by East Bankers. The atmosphere tightened, and Palestinians sensed their separation more. An East Bank attitude that had been little voiced now became more open: Jordan was the East Bank and should wash its hands of the Palestinian problem. Prince Hassan was said to be sympathetic to this viewpoint.

Ultimately the atmosphere eased again, once more as a consequence of outside events. The rapprochement of the King and the PLO leadership, beginning in 1979, led to the 1984 meeting in Amman of the PLO's legislative body, the Palestinian National Council. It became less difficult to be both a Palestinian and a Jordanian.

The easing of domestic relationships had an economic basis as well with origins beyond Jordan's borders—the economic boom in the oil countries of the Persian Gulf, in the late 1970s and into the 1980s. The extraordinary economic expansion of this period provided a plentitude of jobs, in Jordan and in the Gulf states themselves. Job competition and insecurity ceased to be an immediate irritant in relations between Palestinians and East Bankers. The rapid development of the private sector in Jordan, long a stronghold of Palestinians, gave that group a firmer sense of belonging and at the same time a greater stake in the system. Today, with cutbacks in oil profits dominating Gulf economies, the question looms whether the moderating social effects in Jordan will also be reversed.

The Relationship Today

One fact seems beyond question. Jordanians still identify themselves and others of their countrymen as either Palestinians or East Bankers. It is one of the things a Jordanian would know about everyone he deals with. What is not so clear is how much it matters.

Nor is what people say or even think about their attitudes always a reliable guide to how they will react when the chips are down. A certain litany grows up in describing a situation over the years, and it can change more slowly than the situation itself.

Palestinians, at least those in their middle years or older, no doubt continue to share a sense of grievance. They still seem to feel themselves not quite as fully Jordanian as East Bankers are, a sense, however elusive, of being in someone else's country. They may retain a sentimental attachement to homes in Palestine and a wish to return that is probably more a desire to go back in time than to return to their homes as they are now. A Jordanian sociologist recounts a conversation with a Palestinian who owns a grocery and several buildings in Jordan. "He said to me: 'You know, doctor, just let them find a way for Palestinians to go back and I'll go.' Here he is, better off economically than in his Palestinian village, but he still feels incensed at being thrown out. He is sitting here waiting for a settlement."

The ambiguity they feel about their lives in Jordan gives them a sense that their future is "on hold." It is not decisively resolved, though most of them (we are still talking about the middle-class Palestinians) probably cannot imagine a future other than remaining where they are. Given their numbers, this ambivalence lends a certain tentativeness to the future of the country as well.

Whatever estrangement they feel toward Jordan is usually explained in terms of attitudes they sense on the part of East Bank Jordanians. Palestinians speak of the discrimination and distrust they encounter. Top ranks in the military are closed to Palestinians, as are officer positions in certain security-sensitive combat units. The highest levels in some government ministries are similarly beyond their reach. A Palestinian remarks that most of the top lawyers are Palestinians, but most of the judges are East Bankers. Some Palestinians think they are observed more closely by the security forces than are East Bankers. They fear that if jobs become scarce, East Bankers will have preference.

The Palestinians are right in sensing some distrust by at least the more conservative East Bankers. A senior army officer, himself an East Banker, admits that "quite frankly, East Bankers do worry about being outnumbered by Palestinians, but we know the Palestinians are making a good deal of money and don't want to risk that." Within the army, he says, "we have to watch them because we remember 1970." This officer talks about Palestinians as a different kind of people. "They have a talent for making money that East Bankers do not have. They are traders, merchants, like the Lebanese. If we had to rely on our business skills, we'd starve."

Despite the distinctions that persist, the Palestinian middle class has made a very comfortable home for itself. More than that, it has built an urban society very much in its own image, a society in which it feels comfortable, in some ways more comfortable than conservative East Bankers. Palestinian striving for education and advancement, for example, and their spirit of enterprise have set the tone of Amman society today. The "old country" of Arab Palestine, so much more advanced than Jordan when the first refugees came in 1948, is now a backwater left far behind the burgeoning modernization of Jordan.

Moreover, even when politics was pulling the two groups apart, other processes remained at work that drew them together. Children have attended the same schools, young men have served in the same army. Some students of the issue in Jordan say that younger people are less concerned about the distinctions, about where their elders came from, than is the generation now running things. Many Jordanians comment on the frequency of intermarriage between the groups. There are no statistics on this basis, but some remark that there is hardly a family that is purely East Banker or Palestinian.

During the past few years of easier relations between the government and the PLO, together with the relaxing effect this has had in the country generally, the homogenizing process has had the chance to work more effectively again. With some years' time and a continuation of this conducive climate, a generation could come to maturity that is as much Jordanian as it is either East Banker or Palestinian. Whether the King's break with the PLO leadership in February 1986 will reverse this process remains to be seen.

Camp dwellers are another matter. They came for the most part from rural villages or the poorer areas of the cities. Bound to the land, or shuffled under in urban societies at home, they have not been able to make the transition. Until the boom years beginning in the late 1970s they were mostly unemployed; but the boom has trickled down, and now almost all who want to work are employed. They remain nevertheless the most embittered and the most dissatisfied. Radical PLO groups and the Moslem Brotherhood are said to have far more following in the camps than among Palestinians generally. In the Salt district during the 1984 by-elections, a Christian candidate who aligned himself with the radical Democratic Front for the Liberation of Palestine is said to have gotten most of his support from camp refugees. In Irbid, in the north, on the other hand, camp refugees are thought to have supported strong Islamic candidates.

The unhappy fact is that the camps show no signs of disappearing. Quite the contrary, limited as they are to the original allotments of land, they have been built more and more densely over the years as their populations have increased. It is hard to determine what percentage of the younger refugees manage to break out, but it seems evident that more stay than leave. Fifty percent of the camp population is under twenty years of age.

Baqa'a camp outside Amman is in most respects a typical refugee camp. It was set up in 1968 to house refugees from the 1948 camps in the Jordan valley, on the West Bank, who had fled a second time as the Israelis occupied the territory in 1967. The camp is divided physically into units of 100 square meters, one for each family. At one time five people, on the average, lived in each unit. Now the number has doubled, both from natural increase in the population and from refugees moving from elsewhere to live with their families.

There is an atmosphere of crowding and bustle in the camp. Dust hangs in the air over the streets and lanes, some paved, some not. These refugees are mainly from the West Bank cities of Jerusalem, Nablus and Hebron. People from the same city live together, with their municipal leadership, in sections of the camp known by the names of the cities. Many women wear the native costume of their home regions, and the entire camp has the look of a poorer quarter of a West Bank town. Virtually all the men leave the camp to work, now that work is available, some by the day in nearby jobs, others for longer periods at greater distance. Most work as laborers, though now there are some with better jobs in offices.

Camp dwellers have from the first resisted "being swallowed up in Jordan," as an official of the U.N. refugee agency puts it. The Jordanian government, he says, wants on the other hand to eliminate the camps and the special refugee schools they provide in order to break down these "strongholds of Palestinian nationalism." Jordanian authorities are extending city sewer and electrical systems to the camps, against the bitter resistance of the refugees in some cases. Another refugee official comments, however, that after the peace treaty negotiated between Egypt and Israel at Camp David in 1978, refugees in the camps began to feel they should make the best of their new lives, that they were not going to be able to go back to their homes. To them, according to this official, Egypt's separate peace meant that there would never be a just settlement of the Palestinian problem. But this seems at most to be the start of a slow process of changing outlook.

In talking to refugees one realizes that it makes a difference whether they come from what is now Israel—pre-1967 Israel, as it is called—or from the occupied territories of the West Bank or Gaza. When names of Palestinians were being considered in the summer of 1985 to participate with Jordanians in the first steps of negotiations looking toward a peace settlement, a refugee from pre-1967 Israel was concerned that any delegation contain Palestinians from that area, not just West Bankers or Gazans. He knew that any territory the Palestinians might gain as a homeland from a peace settlement must be in the West Bank and Gaza. To him this was not home, and it would not satisfy him as it might a refugee from there. His problem was different. He needed compensation for the home he left in Israel, a home he realized he would never recover.

In a region long plagued by communal strife, Jordan is a relatively trouble-free society. Aside from Palestinian-East Banker relations, it has no rancorous communal issues. It does not have difficult minority problems, as Syria and Iraq do, or tribal religious hostility as in Lebanon. Perhaps the newness of the society is partly responsible.

A Christian community of some 125,000 is generally well-integrated into the society. Partly at least because of higher educational standards in the past, Christians, like Palestinians, have flourished. They figure out of proportion to their numbers in business and the professions.

At the peak of enthusiasm for the Khomeini revolution among Muslims throughout the Middle East, there were some tensions with Christians in Jordan, but not many. Article 2 of the Jordanian Constitution states that Jordan is a Muslim country, and some criticism of the government was voiced during this period for not implementing the provision vigorously enough. A few liquor stores, owned mainly by Christians, were burned in 1980–81, reflecting the Islamic prohibition on drinking alcohol. Two churches had windows broken, including a new church in suburban Amman where a statue of the Virgin was also smashed. In the latter case church leaders complained to the King, who repaired the damage at his own expense and guaranteed no future trouble.

More recently, in early 1985, a bizarre affront upset Christians in the northern city of Irbid. Four dogs, which are regarded by Muslims as especially unclean and offensive, were found hanged over tombs in the Christian cemetery. At about the same time, in a town near Irbid, the mosque sermon one Friday, broadcast all over town, included an attack on the Christian concept of the divinity of Christ. The local Greek Orthodox Bishop came to Amman to complain and was received by the Prime Minister.

Excesses such as these are usually ascribed to the Muslim Brotherhood, which also took it on itself to have hotels in Jordan abandon the practice of holding the traditionally alcoholic New Year's Eve parties. Christian churches continue to program a church service on Jordanian government-run television every Sunday from 9–10, however, and interconfessional peace is the norm in the country.

More important perhaps, in this day of turbulence among Islamic sects, the Muslim population of Jordan is almost entirely Sunni, the mainstream branch of Islam. There are virtually no Shiites in the country and consequently little sectarian foothold for the militant Islamic movement radiating out of Shiite Iran into Jordan. Jordan thus does not have the concern of Iraq, with its large Shiite population but Sunni leadership. There is also no counterpart of the Alawite minority sect that has dominated Syria politically for so many years.

The most notable Muslim minorities are primarily ethnic rather than religious: the Circassians and Shirhanis. The 25,000 Circassians are Sunnis and the 2,000 Shirhanis are Shiites (among the few in Jordan). Their role in the country springs from their non-Arab origins. Coming from Caucasia in the 1880s, the Circassians especially were used by the Turks as loyal instruments of empire among the Arabs. They have in a sense continued to play this role for the Hashemites and are found in disproportionate numbers in the government and in the military and security services. Elaborately costumed Circassians form a ceremonial guard in the Palace offices.

Aspects of Modernization

Jordanian society has been subjected to an extraordinary rate of change. Urbanization, the raising of educational levels, the transformation of the more traditional elements in society, and other changes associated with modernization have indeed been dramatic in a short period of thirty years.

As in other developing countries, these changes have produced a certain amount of stress within society. The growing disparity between the traditional form of government and an increasingly modern society is one consequence. The changes, however, have also worked in the opposite direction to ease some of the strains that could have been especially disruptive. Education has been especially important in bringing the East Bank population up to a level more nearly equal to that of the Palestinians. What was once, thirty years ago, a society half-modern and half-traditional has now become a good deal more homogeneous in this respect.

A most revealing set of figures about educational advances was compiled by the Jordanian Statistical Bureau in 1974, when the generation from the early days of the state was still alive. It showed that men born in 1909 or before had an 18 percent literacy rate, while 5 percent of women of the same age bracket were literate. Men born in 1935–39 had a literacy rate of 50 percent; women, 30 percent. Those born in 1960–62, however, had a literacy rate of 83 percent for boys and 80 percent for girls. As a current measure of educational progress in 1974, 98 percent of boys and 93 percent of girls of ten years of age were in school in that year. By 1983, 820,000 Jordanians, one-third of the total population, were students.

A second characteristic of education in Jordan is the determination of parents to put their children through university-level schooling. In 1983–84, 24,000 students were enrolled in Jordan's two universities, the huge, sprawling University of Jordan on the outskirts of Amman and the newer Yarmouk University in the north. A somewhat greater number, 32,000, were enrolled in community colleges. Slightly more than 60,000 students were studying abroad (see Table 1), mostly in Arab countries but also in Eastern and Western Europe and the United States (15,000).

The Eastern European countries, the Soviet Union (4,500 students) and Romania (2,890) especially, have acquired a significant role in Jordanian higher education by offering financial incentives to those who cannot afford the more expensive schools of the West. Another form of incentive, less spoken of, seems to be that one can arrange to obtain a Romanian degree without actually studying very hard. Students returning to Jordan with their Eastern European degrees have trouble getting jobs, however. Not only is the education they have received little regarded in Jordan, but the Eastern European language they learned in the process is of no value in business. Schooling in the West, especially the United States, is much preferred on both counts.

But education in Jordan has more than social value as a factor in the homogenization of society. Human resources are among Jordan's few natural advantages. A skilled and educated work force is a major export commodity. It helps pay the bills for the country's imports. It is also a key resource in building a service economy at home that can provide Jordan a profitable economic role in the region even in the absence of natural resources.

Another common measure of modernization is a population shift from the land to the cities. A rough indication of the transformation that has occurred in Jordan is the comparison between population

TABLE 1
Jordanian Students in Higher Education in Other Countries, 1982–83

United States	15,000
Lebanon	9,830
Egypt	8,350
Soviet Union	4,500
Romania	2,890
Syria	2,726
Yugoslavia	2,320
Iraq	1,630
Spain	1,545
Saudi Arabia	1,521
West Germany	1,404
Italy	1,295
Other	7,185
Total	60,196

Source: Jordanian Department of Statistics, *Statistical Year Book 1983*.

figures of the late 1920s and those of the 1979 census. In the earlier period, during the formative days of the country, the total population was less than 300,000, nearly half of whom were bedouin. The five main towns housed a total of 54,000, or a little over 16 percent of the total. By 1979 roughly 60 percent of Jordanians lived in urban areas. The cities themselves have grown immensely. Amman was a town of 20,000 in the late 1920s; in 1983 it had a population of 744,000. Irbid, to the north along the road to Syria, grew in the same period from 3,000 to 131,200.

In one important respect, of course, the figures are misleading. The growth of the cities has not resulted solely from movement into them from the countryside. As we have noted, the Palestinian refugees were already a considerably urbanized people when they arrived in Jordan. It is they who have been mainly responsible for the vast expansion of the Amman urban area. Nonetheless, the picture of a country transformed from a largely rural to a highly urban one is valid and significant, whatever the process.

Amman is the hub of the new Jordan. It is a new city on an old site. An amphitheater built into a downtown hillside is all that remains of the Roman city of Philadelphia. A small trading settlement existed here at the time of World War I. The growth that began shortly thereafter, when Abdallah picked the place for his capital, came in stages that reveal themselves like rings in a tree. The early sections are packed densely on the hills in what is now the eastern end of town. The buildings are undistinguished cement boxes, clinging, many of them, to improbably steep hillsides. The streets are narrow and jammed with motorized traffic—another measure of modernization: annual registration of motor vehicles climbed from 24,279 in 1970 to 197,783 in 1983, growing by almost a third each year during the mid-1970s. The poor live here, in East Amman, in slums that seem poorer than ever as the upper class districts of West Amman have become richer and richer.

Toward the west, the districts are identified by the names of hills (jebel): Jebel El Hussein, Jebel El Luweibida, and the well-to-do Jebel Amman. The best residential areas are strung out on Jebel Amman and beyond, along an avenue broken by a series of traffic circles. These circles, in turn, identify the neighborhoods, with a Dantean twist. One lives near the second circle, for example, or the third or the fifth. The American Embassy is near the third circle; there is a fifth circle pharmacy.

Close to the center of the city, along streets lined with trees, are neighborhoods of relatively modest villas built up in the 1950s and 1960s. Farther out, at the fifth, sixth and seventh circles, lies a residential frontier territory, product of the recent boom years. The new suburbs of Abdoun and Shmeisani are especially fashionable. Raw new villas, some of large size and doubtful taste, some with clean and elegant lines, have sprouted up along unpaved streets and intermittent sidewalks. This is the land of the Mercedes 200. New shopping centers are opening on the ground floors of buildings that, a story or two higher up, are still under construction. And among the villas and the supermarkets, where the native rocky pastureland shows through, the children of rural families arrive in the morning to graze their flocks of sheep and goats as the commuters head for jobs in town.

One aspect of modernization has touched the soul of the country more than the familiar processes of urbanization and education. Jordan's tribes, once half the population and always an essential element in the character of the society, have begun to lose their power and authority. Those that were nomadic, and not all were, have largely been settled. In the late 1970s only about 3 percent of the population was still nomadic. More important is the breakdown of tribal allegiances. Kamel Abu Jabber, former Director of the Center of Strategic Studies at the University of Jordan, finds that the "extended family, the tribe, and the village elder as a form of social organization and security are being replaced with bureaucrats, professional associations and modern business and interest groups. . . .More and more," he says, "individuals are thinking in terms of wife and children, not even of father and mother"—the nuclear family.[1] These processes may be in relatively early stages, but they have already had important effects.

Weakening of the tribes has more than social significance. The tribes and leading families have been reservoirs of support for the Hashemite monarchy. Loyalties have been ensured by allocating major military and political positions to tribal and family members. As tribalism diminishes, these systems of control, this basis of loyalty to the king, lose their effect. To the extent that the state is heir to the loyalties once owed to the tribe, of course, a new kind of bond is being forged. The state, after all, has promoted the social and economic changes that are responsible for this evolution. Jordan is becoming—has become—a welfare state. The public has increasingly demanded services in fields such as health, education and welfare. To meet these demands and to compete with other political movements in the region, the state has come to play major roles in these aspects of life as in the economy and the media.

The King and his government thus have a new and potentially more cohesive system of allegiance to work with—growing identification of the public with Jordanian nationality and a Jordanian state. But to exploit it fully may require different techniques and a more modern approach to governing, a difficult path for this government to follow.

The process of modernization, and the clash of old ways and new, is nowhere more evident than in the role of women in Jordanian society. In pre-1948 Jordan the status of women was defined largely by traditional custom. Few women were seen on the streets, and then only veiled. Women in the workplace were virtually unheard of except

---

[1]Kamel Abu Jabber, "Change and Development in Jordan," in *The Contemporary Mediterranean World*, Carl F. Pinkele and Adamantia Pollis, eds. (New York: Praeger, 1983), pp. 39, 31.

for teachers and nurses.

Into this traditional setting came the Palestinians. In their more urban, more secular culture women had already begun to break out of the conservative mold. They tended to recreate on the East Bank the kind of society they had before, including the place of women. Jordanian culture, fortunately, did not run to fanaticism on this or other subjects, and what occurred, rather than violent confrontation, was the existence of two patterns side by side.

In time the East Bank Jordanian pattern began to change, led and prodded by the Palestinians. We have seen above the figures on education, showing the remarkable opening up that took place for women in the 1960s and 1970s. The 1970s saw efforts by the government to accelerate the process of change. Since 1976, conferences have been held to draw attention to the issue of women in society and encourage their participation in economic and public life. They were given the right to vote and hold office in 1974, though with the hiatus in political activities, the first national elections in which they voted were the parliamentary by-elections of 1984.

But there remains a significant gap between the modern and conservative patterns. Palestinian women still tend more to venture out individually into jobs in private industry. The women of East Bank families typically move into the government, where jobs are found for them in the traditional way by a family member. Or, in the smaller towns and villages, they go to work in groups, bussed to factories producing pharmaceuticals—as in the city of Salt—or clothing, biscuits, and other consumer goods.

Efforts to close the gap between the two patterns, and to improve the climate of women's rights generally, are private as well as official. The Professional and Business Women's Club, for example, works at various levels with women's problems. Two hundred members, presided over by the wife of a former Minister of Labor and Social Development, run a Consultation Center for Women in Amman to advise women on marital, legal, economic and other problems. The Center tries to find jobs for women and creates cottage industry employment for poorer women, providing cloth and thread for those who can sew at home and selling the things they make. It instructs women about their rights, especially widows and women involved in divorce or separation.

The Sharia legal code of the Islamic faith, derived from the Koran, gives women many rights. But a society still dominated by men does not always make it easy for women to know what their rights are. The

Club works with the Sharia courts to make sure that women are aware of the protections they are due. The Club is also working with the Sharia court system on amending the civil laws on the rights of women prior to the process of moving the amendments through Parliament. The mufti (religious judge in the Sharia court system) is cooperative and participates in meetings to brief the women.

Jordanian society is a mixed picture of cohesion and conflict, of growing together and remaining apart. Some say the greatly widened rich-poor gap is the most likely social cause of serious unrest, if it comes. More often the presence of a Palestinian majority in the population is cited as the major question mark for the future of the country.

For now, Jordan seems to be handling the internal pressures fairly well. The mixture does not appear to be an inherently explosive one. Nevertheless, the strains in Jordanian society are vulnerabilities that increase the risks attached to any untoward eventuality. The death of the King, ultimately inevitable, is one challenge that will measure the cohesiveness and maturity of the society. Meanwhile, failure of the monarchy to deal effectively with serious internal or regional pressures, especially those that spring from the Palestinian problem, could strain the seams that bind the society together.

Barring some untoward event, it does not appear that the Palestinian-Jordanian population of the country poses a threat to the monarchy. Looking at a rounded picture of Palestinians in Jordanian society today, one does not get the impression that they harbor intentions of taking over the country and making it the "Palestinian state." Quite the contrary, they would see this as solving Israel's problem, not their own. They no doubt would realize that converting the country into the Palestinian state would mean giving up whatever claims they have to what most regard as their true homes. If they have any common attitude toward Jordan, it is precisely that this is not their home. Moreover, it is the most radical among them—those that would be expected to press hardest for extreme measures—who are most committed to return and most resistant to the idea of staying in Jordan. To the extent that some might want to intervene radically in Jordan (the PFLP, for example), it would be to enlist Jordan in pan-Arab efforts to regain the Palestine they lost, as the PFLP tried to do in 1970. Finally, Palestinians living in Jordan, if the idea did occur to them, would be aware that the power of the army and the security forces would be arrayed against any attempt to replace the monarchy. They can have no illusions about the chances of prevailing against those odds.

Before middle-class Palestinian-Jordanians would abandon their present role in society and attempt to take over the state in some radical way, the basic context would have to change for them. As one example, unlikely but conceivable, the King might give up on the Palestinian problem after a failed attempt at a peace settlement and try to "Jordanize" his kingdom, making the Palestinians give up their dual identity, eliminating the dual representation in the Parliament, and so forth. If Palestinians felt they had nothing to wait for any longer, that the present situation was "it" for the long pull, that they were stuck with Jordan for good, they might then see advantage in taking direct control. Perhaps, even then, they would want to do so while retaining the monarchy. But the general satisfaction of most of them with life in Jordan now would be a restraining influence. Few certainly would want to see the quarreling PLO factions move in to fight over the government of a Palestinian state. Palestinians with less commitment to the status quo, principally those in refugee camps, are much farther from the levers of power and carefully controlled by the security forces.

4

The Army:
Backbone of the Monarchy

A t five o'clock on the morning of September 17, 1970, troops from
the Jordanian 1st Infantry Division and 4th Mechanized Division
assaulted Amman from the north and east. The war against the PLO
militias had begun. It was to be a severe and important testing of the
Jordanian army both politically and militarily—politically, because the
army of a country with a Palestinian majority, itself having about 40
percent Palestinians in its ranks, was being turned against what was,
in effect, the army of the Palestinians; militarily because the army was
faced early in the struggle by a large-scale Syrian invasion, intended to
support the Palestinian militias. The army was forced to fight both
internal and external threats.

The Jordanian monarchy went through a few dark days. King
Hussein was quoted as saying it was "the most harrowing experience
of my life." In all the army's engagements over the years, only this
once would its defeat have exposed the monarchy to destruction and
the integrity of the country to compromise. Facing both inward and
outward, it was playing the dual role that gives it such decisive importance for the future of the monarchy and the country.

Rooting Out the PLO, and the Syrian Invasion

The assault on the PLO forces in Amman went slowly. The Palestinian militias were deployed among the stone and cement buildings
densely packed on the steep hillsides of the poorer sections of down-

town Amman and in the refugee camps concentrated around the city center. They were well armed with Soviet designed automatic rifles, machine guns, antitank grenades and mortars. They fought, moreover, in heavily populated areas crowded with Jordanian civilians, imposing restraints on the kind of force the army could use.

By the morning of September 20 the army had fought through to the hard core of the old city sections. Stiff fighting seemed still to lie ahead. At this point, however, the Syrians attacked, and the focus of battle shifted to the north.

On the eve of the Syrian attack the PLO had been in a strong position in the principal northern cities, none of which is far from the Syrian border. When the fighting had started in Amman on September 17, the PLO had taken control of Irbid, the major city in the north and the third largest in Jordan. Their strength in this area, moreover, so far as Jordanian tactical considerations were concerned, was augmented by the presence of the 15,000-man Iraqi force in Jordan, including an armored division located northeast of Amman. Iraq was known to sympathize with the PLO, and Jordanian commanders could not be certain whether this force would intervene on the side of the Palestinians. Iraq, in fact, had warned Jordan in early September that it would intervene if the Jordanians continued the shelling of PLO positions that was then occurring.

The first indication of trouble from Syria, as it turned out, had been the redeployment of the Iraqis to the east, clearing the way for Syrian movement southward from the border toward Amman. On learning of the Iraqi shift, King Hussein had ordered some of the armor he had available in the north—from the Jordanian 2nd Division—to take up positions behind the crest of a long north-south ridge that commanded the valley of Ramtha, through which the major north-south routes pass.

The Syrian attack came at 5 a.m. on September 20, when the lead units of the Syrian 5th Infantry Division crossed the border at the city of Ramtha. Reinforced with armor and accompanied by a brigade of the Palestine Liberation Army (the PLA, a military unit of Palestinians stationed in Syria, not a PLO force), it included more than 200 tanks. The Syrians advanced south along Route 15, leading from Ramtha to the old Roman city of Jerash and thence to Amman.

During the early morning of the 20th the Jordanian British Centurion tanks, dug in on the ridgeline, battered the Syrian tank force moving through the valley below. Eventually, however, Syrian numbers told, and Jordanian forces were forced to redeploy southward during the night of September 20-21 to another ridge on the northern slopes of the Ajlun Mountains.

The following day was decisive for the local conflict. The Jordanian airforce was committed against the Syrians massed in the Ramtha valley. The British-made Hawker Hunters played havoc with the enemy's armor, and the Syrian force was unable to break through the hurriedly-prepared Jordanian defensive line. By the morning of September 23 the Syrians had withdrawn back across the border.

The war against the Syrians was short, and only part of it took place on the battlefield in Jordan. While the Jordanian army held the pass, so to speak, the United States and Israel brought strong pressure to bear on Syria. King Hussein appealed to the U.S. government as early as September 20 for U.S. air attacks on the advancing Syrian force. The United States had already requested Soviet cooperation in restraining the Iraqis in early September, and had taken some precautionary and warning measures when the conflict began with the PLO, moving Sixth Fleet units into the Eastern Mediterranean. Washington believed, however, that Israel was in a better position than the United States to intervene directly with air support, and it worked closely with the Israelis during the crisis. The United States also pressed the Soviet Union to restrain Damascus. Hussein was not attracted to the idea of Israel's intervention, especially as the Israelis believed they would have to move on the ground as well as in the air. Ultimately Jordan needed no outside military support, but Israel's putting its airforce on alert and mobilizing its armored forces on the Golan Heights no doubt put considerable pressure on Damascus.

Syria's failure to commit its own airforce was of major importance. Hafez el-Assad (now the Syrian President), at that time Defense Minister and airforce commander, withheld his aircraft from an operation he apparently did not concur in. With its superior air power Syria could have made it costly for the Jordanians to fight from the static tank defense line on September 20, and it would have been virtually impossible for the small Jordanian airforce to operate on September 21. Jordanian vulnerability in the air was demonstrated in a sense by the very success it achieved without enemy aircraft to contend with. In general, the Syrian invasion was ill-conceived, hastily prepared, and poorly carried out. Jordan could not count on being that lucky again.

With Syria out of action, Jordanian attention returned to the domestic front and the entrenched PLO militias. The PLO hold on Irbid was broken after a week of fighting by troops from the 2nd Division. In Amman the remaining PLO strongholds were isolated and sealed off by the end of September. While the Palestinian militias remained in Jordan for the time being, the hold they once had had on the country was broken. Over the next months their positions were gradually picked off by the army until they were isolated in a mountain defensive complex in the forest of Ajlun, in the north. There they were attacked in the final act of the conflict on July 13, 1971. After four days of fighting the struggle was over. The last elements of the PLO militias disintegrated, some fighters slipping across the borders into Syria or Lebanon, some crossing to the West Bank, others disappearing among the Jordanian population. About 2,300 were imprisoned; most were soon released to leave the country or go back to a peaceful life in Jordan, the last being let go under a 1973 amnesty.

The conflict had caused several thousand casualties, mainly among PLO fighters and Palestinian civilians. Great destruction occurred as well, some refugee camps being virtually leveled.

Palestinians in the Jordanian army, close to 40 percent of the total, as noted, had been pressed by the PLO to desert. While most were in technical or less sensitive combat units, rather than those that bore the brunt of the fighting, many must have felt some ambivalence about fighting Palestinian militiamen. In the end a sizable number did desert—perhaps as many as 5,000—some of them going over to the PLO. But the great majority (some 18,000-22,000) stayed and did their jobs.

The Army, Yesterday and Today

Throughout its roughly sixty years the army has made two vital contributions to the Hashemite monarchy. As in 1970, it has supported the King through some pretty thin times at home, and in turbulent and threatening international and regional settings it has provided a credible defense force without which the Hashemite leadership could not have maintained its legitimacy.

The army's role as defender of the monarchy against domestic threats has from the earliest days given special importance to the backgrounds and attitudes of the men who led and manned it. The shift from a non-tribal to a tribal base in 1930 was an early and fundamental example. With the passage of time and the changes in Jordan's population, the makeup of the army has posed sensitive issues for the leadership. In addition, the evolving needs of modern warfare have created a requirement for different capabilities in the men recruited for service.

Since 1948 the most difficult and persistent issue concerning the composition of the army has been the recruitment of Palestinians. The problem arose as soon as the Palestinian issue itself arose for Jordan with the acquisition of the West Bank and responsibility for so many Palestinians in 1948. Agitation commenced almost at once among Palestinians on the West Bank for participation in a military force that would protect them against further Israeli attacks. In time they called also for a force that would recover the territories lost to Israel. A "refugee army" was spoken of. The Jordanians tried to draw off the pressure by heavy recruitment of Palestinians into the National Guard, established in 1950. The Guard consisted of local units, poorly armed and ill-trained. It had little chance of protecting the frontier villages against Israeli raids but might, Amman hoped, give the Palestinians some sense of participation.

This effort largely failed. The government primarily intended the frontier forces to prevent infiltration of Arab guerrillas into Israel, fearing Israeli reprisal attacks. This they did not do, and when the attacks came, notably the bloody Israeli raid on the village of Qibya in October 1953—led, incidentally, by Ariel Sharon—they proved powerless to defend against them. Qibya unleashed violent Palestinian demonstrations against the Arab Legion, at that time still under British leadership, and against the Jordanian government and representatives of Western countries in Amman. There were demands that Glubb be dismissed and the Legion "Arabized."

The recruitment of Palestinians by Egypt (which maintained separate refugee military units) and Syria increased the pressure on Jordan to do likewise. Indeed, much of the pressure was fomented in Cairo and Damascus, which were making every effort to undermine Hashemite rule. Amman feared, however, that such units would lead to even more serious border friction with Israel, a concern that the refugees in turn regarded as further evidence of Hashemite complicity with Israel.

At about the same time, the Arab Legion began to need the technical skills that only the Palestinians had the educational background and experience to provide. Glubb recruited limited numbers, screening and controlling them very carefully. The King was reluctant to proceed rapidly down this road, fearing among other things that it would upset the elements in the army that were loyal to him

Despite the relatively good record of Palestinian officers and men in 1970, the senior army officer quoted as saying "we don't fully trust Palestinians in the army" seems to reflect a common attitude in the largely East Bank command structure. While they are increasingly recruited, therefore, as their proportion in the population has grown, they continue to be largely excluded from positions and units where they could interfere seriously with the army's defense of the monarchy. Their growing numbers, even so, cannot help but affect the character of the army in the years ahead. The percentage of Palestinians in the army, having dropped from about 40 percent to close to 15 percent during the 1970s, is now back up in the 30 percent range.

National conscription, instituted in 1976, has brought in an annual draft of some 20,000 that roughly reflects the population makeup in the country. But most of the conscripts never fully become part of the army. They have a shorter training period than recruits and are given less "military" jobs. In the words of one observer, they tend to become "bag boys and tea servers." Most do not remain in the service after their two years' duty are up. Conscription did, however, have the effect of increasing recruitment, as it was expected to, with men signing up for the regular army for five years at relatively good pay rather than be conscripted for two years at very low pay.

Conscript training is primarily intended to prepare large numbers of young men and women to be the core of a "people's army," a kind of reserve force that has been on paper for many years but has not gotten off the ground. In the minds at least of some in the military command who designed the measure, it was hoped that creation of an effective reserve would make it possible to cut back the size of the expensive standing army. Israel was seen as a model, but at the same time it was recognized that Israel has been the only country to make such a system work with a high degree of reliability. The project moved a notch forward in July 1985 when the lower house of Parliament passed a People's Army Law requiring all men between the ages of 16 and 55, and all women students in secondary and college-level schools, to join a paramilitary reserve force to be trained and supervised by the army.

The army is still drawn predominantly from those sectors of the population that have manned it in past years. The great majority of the senior officers are selected from the principal tribal groups in the country, such as the Huweitat, Beni Saqr, Sirhan, Shamman, Beni Hassan, and Majalis. A balance is maintained among the groups that traditionally play this role so that none has too much strength and none feels discriminated against.

Junior officers and enlisted personnel have also come from these tribal groups and from other tribes and extended families that made up so much of traditional East Bank society. Tribal leaders were at one time rewarded for high levels of recruitment among their followers.

Today these tribes and families are less cohesive than they were. Under the pressures of modernization, many constituent families and individual members have moved to towns or cities from the countryside. With more education the men have gone into the wide variety of jobs offered in a more complex society. Nonetheless, however their circumstances may have changed, these families of traditional background still provide a high proportion of the East Banker military men. In this sense the army is still a heavily bedouin army despite the relative scarcity of true bedouin in modern Jordan.

But recruits now entering the army, even those coming from the same traditional sectors of society, can be assumed to have attitudes toward the army and the country somewhat different from those of their fathers and grandfathers. As tribal and family ties weaken in a modernizing society, the young soldiers would see themselves more as members of a nation and less as tribal members with a first loyalty to the King. But this is a slow process and has probably not made a marked difference as yet. The bond between these soldiers and the King is still very real.

The army also seems to be retaining the other characteristics for which it is noted, principally its high military quality and its strong Western orientation. Military excellence, of course, can be conclusively demonstrated only in battle, and the Jordanian army has a record in which victory and defeat are somewhat evenly balanced. But even in its most catastrophic defeat, in 1967, it fought well enough, overwhelmed as it was by Israeli superiority, especially in the air.

Evident even in peacetime is its high level of training and its discipline. It is a thoroughly professional army, with virtually none of the politics and corruption that so weaken many other Third World forces.

The army is not without its problems, however. It has been plagued for years by morale problems. Soldiers have found it difficult to support their famililies on pay that, low to begin with, has tended to lag well behind inflation. A mutiny flared briefly in the large base at Zarqa in 1975 on this issue. A second problem has been trouble in maintaining equipment of very high technology. Military observers worry that such equipment would tend to break down after a few days of fighting. In this one area the quality of training seems less exemplary.

The Western orientation of the army derives in the first instance from that of the society as a whole. Beyond that, the purely military ties with the West, especially the United States, are strong. Military officers at various stages of their careers train and study in the United States as well as in Britain and Pakistan. Weapons procurement is almost all from the West, and this brings with it training and indoctrination courses in their use and upkeep, either in the producing country or in Jordan. Jordan has obtained anti-aircraft equipment from the Soviet Union, but the basic weaponry that shapes the whole orientation of the force, such as tanks and aircraft, is likely in the future as in the past to come from the West.

Threats and Capabilities

From the period of chaos that followed World War I the Jordanian army has had, in addition to its internal support of the monarchy, the role of defending the state against outside attack. In the 1920s the threat came from the south in the form of Wahabi tribal raids from what is now Saudi Arabia. Since World War II the threats have been from the west and north and have become much more serious.

Against these modern threats Jordan is no longer defensible in strictly military terms. The facts of geography and of comparative military strength are all against it.

The heartland of Jordan, with its major cities, virtually all of its people and its productive farms, is an area only about 40 miles wide by a little more than 100 miles long. It lies in the northwest corner of the country, tucked into the angle formed by the Kingdom's most dangerous neighbors, Syria and Israel. Amman is 23 miles from the border with the Israeli-controlled West Bank and about 40 miles from the Syrian border. Friendlier neighbors, Saudi Arabia and in recent years Iraq, are far away across relatively trackless desert to the south and east. Egypt, not sharing a common border but part of the security neighborhood nonetheless, is also a distance away across the Gulf of Aqaba in the south.

Terrain is of limited help to Jordanians contemplating defense of this heartland. From Damascus to Amman is a relatively easy north-south drive over undulating countryside. There are no serious terrain obstacles on the main routes, though as the 1970 engagement showed the land does afford some useful defensive positions. The Yarmuk River, which marks the boundary with Syria at its western end, creates a deep gorge as it plunges to the Sea of Gallilee, but the main roads and logical invasion routes lie to the east. (The Syrians did manage, however, in 1970 to misdirect a mechanized infantry brigade heading for Irbid so that it ran afoul of this gorge and was stopped in its tracks.)

The situation is better on the western border, where Israeli forces stand just across the Jordan River. The river itself is not much of an obstacle, being narrow and shallow, fordable in places, and crossed by two bridges. Nor is the rich Jordan River valley a problem for an invader. It is absolutely flat and without any defensible depth, being only a few miles wide. It is fully exposed moreover to artillery firing from the Israeli side of the river. The escarpment, however, that rises some 2,500–4,000 feet from the valley floor to the plateau above is a formidable obstacle. Six paved roads lead to the top of it, but they pass through terrain that lends itself to defense. Even so, with the gross disparity in air power between the two forces, with Israeli large-scale helicopter capability, and with the Jordanian army's lack of anti-aircraft defense, Jordan could not hold the slopes against attack.

Facing the Jordanians across these two nearest boundaries are major league military forces they cannot match in numbers or weaponry. Table 2 compares Jordanian, Israeli and Syrian forces in terms of the most vital components of military power. In all categories Jordan is seriously outclassed—in manpower by two to one at a minimum, and the disparity in major weapons sytems is even more marked.

Jordan has been steadily losing ground, moreover, in this competition. In manpower, aircraft and tanks it fell farther behind Israel and Syria between 1974 and 1984. As one example, Jordanian tank strength was 27 percent of Syria's in 1974 but only 15 percent in 1984. Israel and Syria, with the support respectively of the United States and the Soviet

TABLE 2
Comparison of Jordanian, Israeli and Syrian Military Strengths 1984–85

	Jordan	Israel	Syria
Total armed forces	76,300	141,000*	362,500
Main battle tanks	750	3,600	4,800
Combat aircraft	103	555	503
Expenditure per man ($)	7,100	28,368	8,855

*241,0900 within 24 hours of mobilization; 500,000 when completely mobilized.

Source: The Military Balance 1984–85 (London: International Institute for Strategic Studies, 1985).

Union, race to match or outdo each other in weaponry. This has been especially marked with the resupply of Syria by the Soviets after Syrian losses to Israel in 1982 in Lebanon. As Jordanian military leaders see it, this may be a neck-and-neck race for Israel and Syria, but for Jordan it means being farther and farther outdistanced by the Kingdom's two most likely opponents. With its slender resources, and lacking the full support of either superpower, Jordan cannot hope to catch up.

This, then, is the picture so far as military capability is concerned. The King and his military commanders must put together with that an assessment of the intentions and character of Jordan's neighbors, and of the political currents running in the area, to get a sense of potential threats to the kingdom in the period ahead.

Looking north, Jordanians see a Syria that considers itself the dominant power in the northern Arab world—the traditional Fertile Crescent. It believes itself to be the cradle and heart of Arabism. It has always wanted to lead the struggle against Israel but has been faced for much of the period since 1948 with Egyptian competition for that role. Egypt's separate peace at Camp David provided Damascus with the opportunity for unchallenged leadership, a role Damascus does not intend to allow Hussein and the PLO to undercut. In a more general sense, Syria wants nothing to be done in the Middle East without its participation or acquiescence.

A former Jordanian military leader says "some of us fear that Syria seeks a similar hegemony over Jordan as over Lebanon." That may be a longer-term Syrian goal. For the present what is clear is that Damascus will not readily tolerate an independent Jordanian policy that leaves Syria out of account. For, coupled with Syria's determination to dominate is a fear of isolation. The prospect of a Jordanian-PLO negotiation with Israel for the purpose of settling the West Bank question raises this fear in its starkest form. Such a settlement would leave Syria isolated in its continuing conflict with Israel, with the issue of the Golan Heights, captured by Israel from Syria in the 1967 war, still unresolved and unlikely to be.

Syria is not a hypothetical enemy. During the 1950s and 1960s Damascus and Cairo promoted the attempted coup by Abu Nuwar and other army officers in 1957, and blockaded Jordan in 1957–58 in the course of continuing efforts to bring down the monarchy. In 1958 two Syrian MIG fighters attacked the King's De Haviland Dove aircraft being flown by Hussein and his British pilot, Jock Dalgleish, requiring some fancy low-level maneuvering to escape. Another coup attempt followed in 1959 and the assassination of the Jordanian Prime Minister in 1960. Syria backed the PLO in the late 1960s in its challenge to Jordanian sovereignty and, as we have seen, invaded in support of the PLO in 1970. Once again, in 1980, Syrian armor massed on the border. Angered by Jordan's growing friendship with Iraq and by Jordanian support for a Muslim Brotherhood campaign against the Assad government, the Syrian leadership deployed two armored divisions and one mechanized division with more than 800 tanks in apparent preparation for invasion. It took pressure from other powers, this time the United States and Saudi Arabia, to defuse the crisis.

The second major threat, as Jordanians see it, comes from the west, across the Jordan River. It may seem odd to Americans, and to most Israelis, that Israel is seen as a threat by an Arab country. Israel's goal is widely assumed to be to live in peace with its Arab neighbors, a goal that is perceived to be frustrated by Arab hostility, not by Israeli aggressiveness. Jordanians see it differently. They regard Zionism as being open-ended in its geographic claims and are aware that revisionist Zionism, endorsed by many of the Israeli Likud politicians still prominent in the Israeli government, considers that parts of Jordan belong to Israel's territorial heritage.

Jordanians are particularly concerned at sentiments in Israel favoring a "solution" to Israel's Palestinian problem at the expense of Jordan. They are familiar with the concept articulated by prominent Israelis that "Jordan is Palestine," as well as the calls by some Israelis for the ejection of all Arabs from the area controlled by Israel. Some are aware as well of the theory, advanced in support of such a solution, that the British Mandate was divided at the Jordan River and that that should remain the only division—a Jewish state on the west and a Palestinian state on the east.

While the threat posed by such proposals is not immediately military, to carry them out and impose them on Jordan and the region generally would require military superiority and a readiness to exercise it. The aggressiveness involved in the schemes themselves as well as in a readiness to impose them is considered by Jordanians to be characteristic of Israel. Jordan suffered innumerable military attacks by Israeli forces in the years prior to 1970. To the Israelis, these were for the most part thought of as retaliation and punishment for the use of Jordanian territory by Palestinian guerrillas raiding Israel. Designed to force the Jordanian government to clamp down on these raids, the attacks did achieve this. But they also kept alive such bitter hatred of Israel among

Jordanians, especially the Palestinians, that they at one time compromised the King's capacity to control the raiding and in general to pursue a policy of accommodation with Israel.

The extreme violence of some of the Israeli attacks, with Arab casualties out of all proportion to the losses suffered by Israelis from the Palestinian raids, was meant to and certainly did convey to Jordanians an impression of ferocity and aggressiveness.

The Jordan River line has been relatively quiet since 1970. The memories of past Israeli attacks, reinforced as they are by the Israeli invasion of Lebanon, are important mainly because they lend credibility to Jordanian fears of the more extreme future scenarios. The King, of course, has had another way of measuring the Israelis in his secret meetings with their leaders over the years. Such contacts can temper unjustified Jordanian concerns and, in the absence of a peace treaty, could be important in the future to help ensure that intentions on both sides are correctly understood.

Jordan is also sensitive to its position as a wedge between Israel and Syria. Should war occur between these two states, always a possibility if not a likelihood, Jordan would be uncomfortably close to the action. The routes between Israel and Syria that run through Jordan are not ideal from a military standpoint, but they exist. Even a fear on one side or the other that they might be used could lead, Jordanians worry, to invasion of Jordanian territory for defensive purposes.

It is relevant to these concerns, of course, that when Syria together with Egypt attacked Israel in 1973, neither Syria nor Israel did in fact move into Jordanian territory. Even when Jordan sent armored units to join Syrian forces engaged with Israelis on the Golan Heights, the Jordan River boundary remained quiet. To be sure, the Jordanians arrived on the scene after the Syrians were already on the defensive and did not see much combat—though a whole division was sent by the end of the war, only about 75 tanks actually got into action and only 15 were lost. But the fact remains that Israel did not use the occasion to attack Jordanian territory or use it to outflank Syrian.

Turning to the south, Jordan faces Egypt. Under Nasser, Egypt posed serious political problems, but it has never presented a military threat. It seems highly unlikely to be a threat of any kind for the foreseeable future. It enters the Jordanian strategic equation on the plus side. Yet the volatility of the Middle East is such that the possibility of a hostile Egypt somewhere down the road must be kept in mind by the Jordanian leadership.

Saudi Arabia, farther to the south and east, was Jordan's first military opponent in the 1920s. Now, however, it is the one neighboring state that is thought by Jordanians to pose no potential military threat. Saudi armed forces are divided between an army and a national guard, together about the same size as the Jordanian army. The Saudis have some modern equipment though virutally no combat experience in its use. The heart of the country lies hundreds of miles distant across trackless desert from Jordan's cities. And it is difficult to conceive of a scenario that would bring the two kingdoms to military blows.

Finally, to the east, is Iraq. As a "progressive," revolutionary state opposed to accommodation with Israel, it was at one time a threatening presence. Relatively populous, rich, with a large and well-equipped army, it was, during the 1960s and 1970s, a source of concern in Amman. Bogged down in war with Iran, dependent on Jordan for land access, it has for years been no threat. Relations have been good between the two former Hashemite mandates.

Looking to the future, opaque and unpredictable as it is, Jordan cannot afford to make complacent assumptions. As with Egypt, the most obvious threat is the possibility of change in the Iraqi regime. An overthrow of the leadership in Baghdad designed to make way for peace with Iran, for example, could produce an Iraq that would look far less benignly on a Western-associated state like Jordan.

Defense Strategy and Defense Needs

Faced with a situation in which it cannot defend itself militarily against its most likely opponents, Jordan has developed a strategy that is a mix of the political and the military. The defense against the Syrians in 1970 was in effect a working model. The heart of the strategy is to prevent a swift, silent attack that, as one Jordanian senior military figure puts it, could take over the country during the night like a coup. Once that happens, and a power change is made, he observes, the outside world will do nothing. There must be sufficient time to permit Jordan's friends to come to its assistance politically if not militarily. Such a delay can be achieved in two ways. The existence and proper deployment of a Jordanian army obliges a would-be attacker to mobilize its forces in preparation for serious, large-scale combat. That takes time and tips an aggressor's hand. Second, once an invasion is underway, adequate Jordanian forces can delay the advance.

This is a logical and appropriate strategy for Jordan. One of the advantages of its otherwise uncomfortable position as a buffer state is that neighboring countries and powers outside the region have a stake in its independence and integrity. It might not necessarily be "friendly" states that rally to its defense, of course. One not-so-friendly neighbor might bring more effective pressure to bear against another that threatened to take over Jordan than a more distant power could do. Again the 1970 case is illustrative, with Israel's demonstrative military preparations having helped discourage the Syrians at that time.

Jordan's problem is maintaining fighting forces that are not strong enough to defeat or even defend against an aggressor but yet are credible. The legitimacy of a government depends in part on the conviction of its subjects that it can defend them. Some sense of security is essential. A military force, for its part, must have confidence that the government is providing it with the manpower, training and equipment to be an effective fighting organization. An army must believe it has a chance against a likely adversary. A government that disregards this psychological factor, that appears unable to obtain the weapons its troops need, for example, is likely in time to lose the unquestioning loyalty of the military, so especially important in Jordan's case.

For a country like Jordan, small among more powerful adversaries, it is important for the government to show that it has reliable friends outside the region from whom to obtain the weapons and to whom to turn for the support and assistance it clearly will need in certain potential threat situations. This is not only a matter of reassuring its own military, but of maintaining public confidence and backing. It is also important for potential opponents to be aware of this potential support. Moreover, any policies King Hussein hopes to pursue in the region, as in seeking a solution to the Palestinian problem, are to some extent dependent for their success on the status he derives from having reliable and powerful friends. He must cast a bigger shadow than Jordan alone would make.

Jordan's military commanders are aware of many equipment shortcomings, but the one that worries them most is the weakness of its defense against air attack. The competence of Jordan's army in ground combat would be neutralized by the air superiority of any of the kingdom's likely adversaries. Jordan cannot count on an enemy's airforce sitting it out again as the Syrian airforce did in 1970. What Jordan needs are more modern aircraft and more and better land-based anti-aircraft weapons.

This is a gap the government has been trying to fill for many years. The difficulties the King has encountered in doing so illustrate an important weakness in his position in the Middle East, namely, the unreliability of the United States as a powerful friend and supplier of the weapons he needs to maintain a credible military force. Time after time, with respect to air defense weapons and other major equipment, the United States has not responded even to requests its own military establishment considered reasonable. Frequently, though not always, this has been the result of sales being blocked by a U.S. Congress reacting to Israeli pressure.

The sale of Hawk anti-aircraft missiles in 1975–76 was an early example. The U.S. Department of Defense had studied the Jordanian air defense problem and proposed a mix of American-built weapons, including Improved Hawk Missiles. In the course of the negotiations for the sale, the U.S. government and executive departments held the number of batteries at 14 in an effort to avoid arousing Israeli concerns, and 14 were offered to Jordan. Nevertheless, during the spring and summer of 1975 the Congress, having been routinely notified of the impending sale, came under strong pressure from the Israeli Embassy in Washington and from American Jewish organizations to oppose the sale. The Israelis' experience with ground-to-air missiles in the 1973 war had sharply increased their sensitivity to this type of weapon.

The Departments of State and Defense negotiated with congressional staffs and ultimately with key congressmen and senators to work out a compromise at least minimally acceptable to Israel by which some Hawks could be made available to Jordan. In September, as a result, an offer of 14 batteries was conditioned on the missile launchers being fixed in the ground at sites not considered threatening by Israel. King Hussein quite understandably found the whole process, and the nature of the offer, humiliating. He was pressed by the Syrians to turn to the Soviets for his missiles. Finally the United States added significantly to other less important weapons included in the package and the Jordanians accepted it. Another embarrassment arose in that the price of the Hawks had more than doubled during the course of the prolonged negotiations. Saudi Arabia, which was financing the sale, protested but in the end increased its funding to cover it.

Jordan emerged with a system that did not meet its most important needs, since it covered only a limited area over and around Amman and the air bases to the east of Amman. Even there the number was so limited and their vulnerability so great in the very visible fixed sites that they provided little security.

Some other notable examples followed in subsequent years. Jordan asked to buy F-16 aircraft in 1979. The U.S. government held up any definitive response because of a new worldwide arms sale policy designed to reduce the amount of weaponry exported by the United States. Later that same year King Hussein bought Mirage fighters from France instead.

Complex U.S. restrictions on tank sales led Jordan in 1980 to buy British tanks and to accept an offer from Iraq to supply a number of British and American tanks captured from Iran. The Jordanians made a much-reduced purchase of U.S. tanks because of disagreement about the number of tanks involved and because of initial U.S. unwillingness to sell its M-60 tank with various items of modern equipment the Jordanians considered important, such as night sights, as part of a policy to control export of tanks and tank technology.

When Jordan encounters problems with the United States, there is an obvious temptation to turn to America's political competition, the Soviet Union. The temptation arises not primarily because the Soviet equipment is so inherently desirable—though it is much cheaper; in fact, the Jordanians usually shop in Western Europe as a serious alternative to the United States. But the Soviets represent a way to point a political moral for Washington, namely, that the United States has a stake in Jordan just as Jordan needs it. On occasion, however, Hussein has bought Soviet equipment. He contracted for anti-aircraft missiles in 1981 after the United States had turned down an order for American-made Roland missiles. A more recent purchase of division-level air defense weapons from Moscow was announced in Amman in 1985 following the U.S. refusal to sell Stinger anti-aircraft missiles in 1984.

Jordan's Strategic Role

The U.S. government has understood, over the years, the importance of Jordan in the Middle East equation. It has tended at times, however, to see Jordan's position more through American—and, to be frank, Israeli—eyes than with real sensitivity to the Jordanian perception of it. The Reagan Administration in its early days entertained the curious notion that Jordan should, and would, join a strategic consensus with Israel and possibly other "status quo" states in the Middle East to help the United States keep radicalism and the Soviets at bay. As a Jordanian puts it, "We both know what the U.S. means by strategic. The U.S. means that Jordan will somehow cooperate with Israel to see that the area is not changed." This misguided U.S. concept, and the gross misreading of Middle Eastern priorities and relationships it reflected, has in the main been abandoned. There is now a greater understanding again in Washington of the strategic role Jordan does in fact play. As the same Jordanian continues, defining the Jordanian view of strategic defense, "For Jordan the term means to share the responsibility for the defense of the region, especially with countries that share its objectives and ideology, Saudi Arabia and the other Gulf states in particular."

Jordan has for many years helped the Persian Gulf states build reliable military forces. As the practice has developed, the host government asks for a specific number of military men from Jordan. The Jordanian army transfers ("seconds," as the Jordanians say) personnel to the Gulf states, which then fits them into its hierarchy and uses them as it sees fit. Jordan and Pakistan have shared this role. The Jordanian military, however, have the advantage of a common language and are familiar with all the equipment, whatever its origin. For these reasons, Jordanians say, their military have a dominant position among advisers. There has been a recent tendency for active duty personnel to be replaced by retired Jordanian military, but either way Jordanians are still active in the Gulf.

The Jordanians have for the most part provided training and advice. From 1972 to 1982 Jordan sent 1,150 officers and other ranks to Gulf states for those purposes, and trained 9,007 officers and other ranks in Jordan. About two-thirds of the Jordanians served in the United Arab Emirates, and Saudi Arabia sent the great majority of the military personnel who trained in Jordan.

Jordan has also sent combat forces into the Gulf area. A Jordanian infantry battalion was despatched to Kuwait in 1961 as part of an Arab task force organized by the Arab League in response to a threatening Iraqi posture. In 1975 a Jordanian special forces battalion, requested by Oman, helped the Omanis deal with an insurgency supported by South Yemen.

More recently, after the brief seizure in 1979 of the main mosque in Mecca by dissident Islamic fundamentalists, King Hussein offered to send a division to reinforce Saudi Arabia's internal security forces. The troops were never sent, but the emergency in Mecca and the King's offer led Jordanian commanders to consider how such a force could be transported and supplied if it ever were needed, there or elsewhere in the Gulf region. Following consultations with the American military the Jordanians proposed the creation of a Jordanian "strike force" and requested transport aircraft from the United States sufficient to move and maintain it. Washington was receptive but made the mistake of trying to keep secret the funds it was intending to make available for the purpose. After a good deal of publicity, opposition from Israel and the U.S. Congress, and embarrassment all around, the plan was dropped. While the Administration was naive to think it could finance such a force without the Israelis getting wind of it, an open and public handling of it would have had serious drawbacks aside from Israel's reaction. The Gulf states are etremely sensitive to any implication that they need the kind of assistance contemplated by the plan, and especially that it would in any way have the fingerprints of either superpower on it.

As Jordan is a bastion of free enterprise among Arab states, it should be no surprise that strategic advice is now being provided by private Jordanians on a contract basis. A former army Chief-of-Staff, General Abdul Hadi Majali, on his retirement from government service in 1983, organized the Middle East Institute for Strategic Studies in association with some non-Jordanians. The Institute takes on requests for studies and advice from other governments—those of the Gulf states, for example—and provides a complete set of responses and recommendations.

General Majali has also set up an organization to provide physical security, in the broadest sense including some degree of intelligence warning, on a contract basis. The Middle East Defense and Security Agency (MEDSA) employs retired Jordanian military personnel, a rich resource of skill and experience, to put in place complete physical security systems, involving around-the-clock guard details where necessary, for organizations in Jordan and other countries. The U.S. Embassy in Amman, for example, has contracted for some services. Majali was appointed Director of Public Safety—national police chief, in effect—in July 1985, but the enterprises continue in his absence.

The Jordanian army is a mature and durable institution, established more than half a century ago. Three generations of Jordanians have led and manned it; in many cases they have come from the same army families. It thus has deeper roots than most armies in the Third World today. It is a highly professional organization. Except for a few aberrational years in the late 1950s it has not been tainted by politics and has not harbored would-be military "presidents" or dictators in the tradition of so many countries, some far older than Jordan.

There has been speculation over the years about where the army's loyalties lie. Is it loyal to the King, to the institution of the monarchy, to the Jordanian state? These are not academic questions. Would it be loyal, for example, to any government that took power in Amman, or does it have a commitment to the Hashemite monarchy?

There can be no long-term answers. The army is changing as the population of Jordan—even the East Banker portion of it—is changing. But the best assessment seems to be that for the next decade or so at least the army will remain at heart an East Bank institution, with loyalties to the King and the social-political status quo of present day Jordan, including the monarchy. Such an army would not stand by and allow the monarchy to be replaced by another form of government. It would not accept without a struggle the overturning of the present establishment, with its preponderance of East Bankers—of which the army higher command is a part—by the Palestinian majority or anyone else. The army would defend present-day Jordan against internal as well external enemies.

Should King Hussein die or be killed, the army would almost certainly act in effect as guarantor of the monarchical succession. Crown Prince Hassan is thought to stand well with the army, himself reflecting some of the East Bank bias of the military leadership. He would presumably be supported as the legitimate successor to the throne. In the hypothetical situation envisioned at the outset of this study, in which both Hussein and Hassan should disappear, the army would likely work together with the civilian leadership to see that another Hashemite succeeded to the throne, either the designated successor, Prince Ali, twelve years of age in 1985, or perhaps the twenty-four-year-old Prince Abdallah if a mature ruler were thought necessary.

5

Economy: Prosperity and Vulnerability

A sign in the supermarket in one of Amman's rich new suburbs reads, in English and Arabic: "We have Thailand and Philippine Foodstuff." This sign says that Jordan, in a sense, has arrived economically. The Thais and the Filipinos for whom the food is imported are servants of wealthy Jordanians (and a scattering of diplomats), who live in the neighborhood. Jordanians themselves are seldom servants these days.

In the restaurant of the Intercontinental Hotel, across from the American Embassy, the traditional Arab waiters are now for the most part replaced by the smiling Rosario and her colleagues from the Philippines. These Asians are among the 120,000 or so foreign workers who have come in over the last ten years to fill the labor gaps in Jordan's booming economy.

A look at the supermarket shelves tells the same story. German canary food, dog food, soy sauce in five sizes from the United States, taco shells and taco sauce, four kinds of Kraft salad dressing, three dozen kinds of German or American shampoo, pumpkin, blueberry, and coconut pie filling from Newark, New Jersey.

Jordan, it is said, is one of the richest poor countries in the world. With a GNP per capita income of $1,912 in 1984, it falls well within the top half of the International Monetary Fund's ranked list of 126 countries (see Table 3 which shows Third World GNPs by regions). In the last few years, however, the boom has petered out.

Jordanians are concerned that hard economic times might bring social and political tensions that the kingdom, and the monarchy espe-

TABLE 3

Third World Per Capita Gross National Product by Region, 1984 (US$)

Middle East	4,310
South America	1,730
Central America	1,620
Africa	700
Asia	310

Source: Kurian, George Thomas, *The New Book of World Ratings* (New York: Facts on File, 1984).

cially, can ill afford. The extraordinary prosperity of the late 1970s made the political problems, which lie close to the surface in Jordan, much easier to handle.

It is also said that Jordan's relative prosperity comes in no small measure from playing a poor hand well. For Jordan, economically speaking, is quite a poor hand. It has few natural advantages. Only 6 percent of its land is fit for growing crops; most of the rest is desert. It has little water, and what rainfall it receives is so fickle that poor harvests are a recurring problem. Phosphates and, to a lesser extent, potash from the Dead Sea are its only important natural resources.

Jordan has traditionally been plagued by three deficits: a budget deficit, a balance-of-payments deficit, and a gap between needed investment funds and available savings (see Tables 4 and 5). They are symptomatic of its very limited economic base. The country has been able to bridge these gaps, but to do so has required continuing foreign subsidies, which have inevitably come with a political price tag. Jordan is far from being self-sufficient.

The establishment of Israel in 1948 put a heavy burden on Jordan's economy—largely agricultural and quite primitive at that time—with the sudden influx of refugees. But it also set in motion a process of development that ultimately changed the character of the economy and made it possible to exploit the opportunities for prosperity offered by the oil boom.

The arrival of so many refugees in 1948 might well have swamped the country. But many of the refugees had the skills and expertise, as well as the capital, to begin the development of a significant trade and

TABLE 4
Jordanian External Public Debt, 1980–84
(*millions of Jordanian dinars*)

	1980	1981	1982	1983	1984	Debt Outstanding 1984
Government debt	275.9	335.9	394.6	520.9	639.3	668.5
Foreign governments	223.7	274.8	302.9	357.2	396.8	400.5
International and regional lending institutions	31.8	47.1	64.3	85.0	98.8	126.9
Foreign banks	17.9	11.7	25.4	76.8	142.1	139.4
Foreign commercial companies	2.4	2.3	2.1	1.8	1.6	1.6
Government-Guaranteed debt	95.7	204.9	228.9	288.8	314.0	310.1
Total	371.5	540.9	623.5	809.6	953.3	978.6

Source: Central Bank of Jordan, *Monthly Statistical Bulletin,* July 1985.

TABLE 5
Jordanian Exports and Imports, 1980–84
(*millions of Jordanian dinars*)

	1980	1981	1982	1983	1984
			Exports		
Iraq	28.3	63.5	66.6	26.0	67.8
Syria	13.6	10.7	8.4	3.6	2.9
Saudi Arabia	19.7	20.9	27.6	35.2	38.7
Kuwait	35.3	6.8	6.7	10.4	11.6
India	8.0	10.3	16.6	13.7	34.1
Total exports	120.1	169.0	185.6	160.0	261.0
			Imports		
Syria	10.5	12.5	10.4	14.0	7.3
Saudi Arabia	114.1	175.8	223.5	210.9	208.8
EEC countries	259.7	339.6	329.6	330.1	319.3
United States	61.6	166.7	144.3	131.0	119.3
Total imports	716.0	1047.5	1142.5	1103.3	1071.3

Source: Central Bank of Jordan, *Monthly Statistical Bulletin*, July 1985

services sector. The country moved gradually away from its limited agricultural orientation. The West Bank, acquired by Jordan at the same time, was at first economically richer and more diverse than the East Bank because of the urban center of East Jerusalem and its extensive tourist industry. The far more limited immigration from Syria a decade or so later also brought capital and talent to enrich the Jordanian economy.

To meet the sudden demands, and also to capitalize on the opportunities, the Jordanian government began during those early years to expand the country's infrastructure. The government itself increased in size and range of activity, including the military services. A major water project in the Jordan valley made possible more extensive irrigation of this warm and fertile region. The gross national product grew briskly at annual rates up to 11 percent until 1967.

In that year, however, everything turned around, and Jordan entered its most difficult economic period. The Six Day War of June 1967 resulted not only in the influx of another wave of refugees but also in the loss of the West Bank and Arab Jerusalem that had accounted for almost a third of the country's GNP. The most productive area left to the kingdom, the Jordan valley, came under continuing Israeli attack in succeeding years as Israel sought to halt PLO raiding and rocketing from Jordan. Many thousands fled to the hills and agriculture fell off sharply. Finally, the war with the PLO in 1970 disrupted the economy directly and through the retaliatory economic actions of other Arab countries, especially Syria. Jordan learned—not for the last time—that its handling of the Palestinian issue can bring serious trouble with its more powerful neighbors.

The Oil Boom

After 1973 the oil boom began in the Persian Gulf region. To paraphrase the saying made popular by President Kennedy, all the boats in the Middle East were lifted on a rising tide of Persian Gulf oil. Jordan was no exception. The shaping of the kingdom's present economy, and indeed of important dimensions of the political and social life as well, have been much affected by oil prosperity. Jordan could only be grateful, but at the same time it could not fail to remark that, once again, its fate was determined by outside events over which it had no control.

The oil tide has reached Jordan in a number of ways. The most important and enduring has been the flow of money—remittances—back into the country from Jordanians who have taken jobs in the Gulf states. These workers are Jordan's main resource and principal export. M. Nuri Shafiq, Secretary General of Jordan's Council of Higher Education, once called "educating and training manpower and exporting it to the Gulf the Kingdom's basic industry."

No one knows exactly how many Jordanians have gone south to the Gulf states to work. There are probably 300,000, mostly Jordanian-Palestinians, now in the region; it is thought that about 160,000 workers are in Saudi Arabia, the rest being scattered through the other Gulf states. They have been sending back, through the banking system, a little more than $1 billion a year. Everyone knows that a good deal more money finds its way back in less official ways, perhaps $500 million or more (one leading Amman banker says "double the official figures").

Jordan is providing the Gulf mainly with skilled, educated, white collar workers. The Deputy General Manager of the Arab Bank (Jordan's most important bank) comments, for example, that there has been a big demand in the Gulf for banking employees. One hundred fifty went from the Arab Bank alone in 1982 as part of what he describes as an "exodus of bank employees" in that year.

Although many more Jordanians work in the Gulf now, the practice itself goes back to the late 1940s. The Gulf states began to need significant numbers of foreign workers at about the same time the Palestine refugee problem created a large floating work force of Palestinians. High salaries were paid in those days to tempt foreigners to live in what were quite primitive conditions. A Palestinian-Jordanian engineer who worked in the engineering office of the Saudi National Guard recalls that even as late as 1965 living conditions in Riyadh, Saudi Arabia, were poor. Salaries in the early days were as high as ten times the going rate for the same jobs at home. Now, with the depressed oil economy, the large number of available workers, and the improved living conditions, three times the home salary is maximum, according to the engineer. Foreign workers have always tended to send their money home, partly because they were not allowed to buy property in the Gulf countries. Ninety percent of the workers stay on indefinitely, he says, since comparable jobs, even for less pay, are hard to find in Jordan. Housing is plentiful in some Gulf cities as well.

How major a contribution the current remittances of $1 billion to $2 billion annually make to the economy is evident when one considers that the total gross national product for 1984 was $4.3 billion.

A second important channel has been the subsidy for Jordan agreed on at the Arab League summit meeting in Baghdad in 1978, following the Camp David agreements between Egypt and Israel. The oil-producing states undertook to pay a total of $1.25 billion annually for ten years to encourage and assist Jordan as a "frontline" state in the conflict with Israel. In this way Jordan benefited from Arab bitterness over what the Arabs saw as Egypt's defection in the Camp David peace settlement. In more immediate terms, of course, Jordan was being encouraged not to join in the West Bank peace process envisioned in the Camp David agreements.

The payments were never made by some of the oil states, and countries that have made them have cut them back considerably. Jordan probably never received more than $1.2 billion a year, and by 1984 the amount had fallen to about $550 million. Nevertheless, these are very substantial sums for an economy the size of Jordan's. They illustrate vividly the costs and rewards that can be attached to policies the kingdom pursues.

Subsidies have always played an important part in Jordan's economic life, and they have always been highly political. The continuing sizable gap between the money the country spends and the money it earns through exports of goods and services and other income has always been filled by foreign aid in some form. Until 1957, when King Hussein cut his ties with Britain, London paid the tab. For a period thereafter the United States played this role. Since 1967 the Arab states have been increasingly the main source of funds (the United States has provided no direct budget support since 1979), the subsidy rising or falling with Jordan's standing in the Arab world. Kuwaiti subsidies were cut off after Jordan drove out the PLO militias in 1970–71, for example, but restored after Jordan sent forces to help Syria in the 1973 war with Israel. Most of the time Jordan was able just to scrape along, but the sums voted in 1978 reflected the extraordinary affluence of the oil states in those days. Fortunately for Jordan, and not surprisingly, Saudi Arabia has been the biggest and most reliable donor, since the Saudis have a considerable stake in Jordan's viability.

Iraq has been a third channel in the flow of Persian Gulf oil wealth to Jordan. Not only did Baghdad participate in the subsidy program, but it turned to Jordan for the supply of extensive goods and services. Jordan developed an active export trade to Iraq in the late 1970s and early 1980s. Agricultural produce was a major component, but small manufacturing enterprises were set up as well for the trade with Iraq.

By 1981 Iraq was by far Jordan's largest market, taking 37.5 percent of the Kingdom's exports. More importantly, though, Jordan provided a vital backdoor for Iraq when the vulnerable Iraqi Gulf ports were threatened and ultimately closed and land routes though Syria were also closed as a result of the war with Iran. Iraq financed development of Jordan's port at Aqaba and of the road net between there and the Iraq border. There was talk of building an oil pipeline to Aqaba.

Augmenting the oil tide was brisk trade and high prices in phosphates. The government had pushed the development of phosphate mining, and in the 1970s it paid off handsomely. Jordan became the world's third largest exporter, with 5 percent of the international market (after Morocco and the United States). Production rose from 1,352,000 tons in 1975 to 4,746,000 tons in 1983. Prices climbed to $50 a ton in 1981 before they started to fall. Phosphates provided 57 percent of commodity exports.

Effects of Prosperity

The effect on Jordan of this sudden wealth has been tremendous. Some measure of how much is involved, for a basically rather poor country, is the 1979 figure for gross national product (GNP). The $2.5 billion in that year, was almost triple the average of the previous five years. By 1984 it had reached $4.3 billion. From 1974 to 1980 the average annual growth in GNP was 8 percent, among the highest in the world. In 1980 and 1981 it soared to 17.1 percent and 12.1 percent, respectively.

But figures are abstractions. What were the consequences that could be felt and experienced by individual Jordanians? What will be the longer term effects on the country?

The most obvious, if not necessarily the most important, sign of the sudden prosperity is the building boom in Amman. The phenomenon itself is not new. In the uncertain world of the Palestinian, investment in Amman real estate has long seemed a prudent anchor to windward. In the early 1970s, a period of hard times in Jordan but quite good times on the West Bank, land and houses in the upper-class sections of Amman were already being bid to exhorbitant price levels. West Bankers especially tended to put any excess cash into building villas in the classier western residential areas of the Jordanian capital.

It was only natural, therefore, that the lush Gulf salaries of the post-1973 prosperity led quickly to an unprecedented building boom. Interestingly, the building splurge has been in part a process of transferring oil money from Palestinians to East Bankers. Since most of the Jordanians working in the Gulf are Palestinians, it is they who have fueled the boom. Most of the rural land around Amman has been owned by East Bank families, however, some of them from quite simple rural backgrounds. Those whose property lay in the path of the avalanche have become rich. Land went, during the height of the boom, for as much as half a million dollars an acre. A group has emerged from the process known locally as "peasant investors," rural people made suddenly rich and looking for ways to invest their money, which they do not always do very wisely.

As the prosperity has leveled off with the stagnation of the oil economies, construction seems to have shifted away from luxury housing to apartment blocks and commercial building. Amman's other, less fashionable, hills have seen their own urban sprawl.

Another consequence of the boom is the consumer society evident in the supermarket described at the outset of this chapter. Jordanians worry about it as they participate in it. The professional woman who returned to Amman in 1973 after living in Lebanon comments that Amman now reminds her of Beirut in 1972: too much money, too much false sophistication, a consumer society. Money has come in, but there is no effective tax system to spread it. Although she does not mention it, others express concern that this burgeoning materialism could feed the Islamic movement. She does say, however, that much as she deplores it, religion is where the true feeling is today in Jordanian society.

The consequences of the oil-fed prosperity have not all been at the consumer level. The economy has expanded in all respects. The service industries have grown especially and make up 61 percent of gross domestic product (GDP) if one includes the government and military services, compared with 29 percent for manufacturing, mining and construction, and 7.5 percent for agriculture (see Table 6).

Employment in the tourism industry has jumped from 2,284 in 1977 to 6,368 in 1983. Hotels, 233 in 1983 as against 145 in 1977, are the principal employers. The number of tourists grew from fewer than 150,000 in 1960 to more than a million annually by 1980, even with the loss of much of the Holy Land tourist trade after 1967. The trend remained upward, but tourism is sensitive to conditions in the area and on the travel routes. It was sharply down in 1985, a year of ship and plane hijackings in the Middle East. Three-quarters of the tourists are Arabs attracted to the relaxed atmosphere and mild climate. Lebanon's bloodletting has been Jordan's gain in this respect; Beirut was at one time a major resort for Gulf Arabs.

Especially important has been the development of a domestic financial system that gives Jordan some cushion against the vagaries of outside financial support. The banking system grew by 25 percent a year from 1974 until 1982 to handle the influx of oil money. The sixteen commercial banks have expanded their operations and have ventured into the investment field. Six new investment banks opened, as well as three Islamic banks based on a profit-sharing principle. Savings and loan institutions have been established, attracting deposits to invest in housing construction.

A bond market has developed in the local currency (the Jordanian dinar, or JD, worth $2.60 in June 1985); through it, local companies can tap a domestic savings pool for investment capital. This savings pool is

TABLE 6
Industrial Origin of Jordanian Gross Domestic Product (at factor cost)
(*millions of Jordanian dinars*)

	1974	1983 (preliminary)
Agriculture, forestry and fishing	30.3	105.4
Mining and quarrying	10.8	37.9
Manufacturing	29.7	176.6
Electricity and water supply	3.0	28.3
Construction	16.8	126.8
Wholesale and retail trade, restaurants and hotels	42.3	210.9
Transport and communications	22.8	136.7
Financing, real estate and business services	25.2	135.6
Community social and personal services	4.3	27.2
Less: Imputed bank service charges	–2.7	–22.2
Producers of government services	54.3	232.0
Non-profit institutions	4.9	20.2
Domestic services of households	0.7	3.5
Total GDP at factor cost	242.4	1236.0
Factor income from abroad	32.0	346.7

Source: Central Bank of Jordan, *Monthly Statistical Bulletin*, July 1985.

apparently being substantially augmented from Jordanian mattresses, long a favored repository of spare cash in troubled times. Commercial banks have linked their resources for large-scale syndicated loans to domestic enterprises that would otherwise have to resort to the Eurodollar market. The first such operation, headed by the government-backed Industrial Development Bank, was an eleven-bank loan in 1979 for $27 million to Jordan's only cement factory.

To the average Jordanian the boom has meant a job and more money to spend. From the 1967 war to 1974 unemployment was a serious problem, causing social tensions, especially between Palestinian and East Bankers. There was concern that it fed radical causes. Prosperity brought full employment. The tens of thousands of skilled workers who went to the Gulf states left gaps to be filled by other Jordanians. At the same time, the flourishing of the local economy created jobs at all levels (see Table 7).

Jordan imported about 120,000 foreign workers, somewhat more than a quarter of the Jordanian workforce. Ninety thousand of them, mostly from Egypt and Asia, fill unskilled jobs, especially in agriculture and construction, while 30,000 are highly skilled Westerners and semi-skilled technicians.

More money has created a new kind of middle class. A member of a prominent Jordanian studies institute comments that this is a middle

TABLE 7
Distribution of Estimated Labor Force in Jordan
by Economic Activity, 1982

Total work force	454,468
Agriculture	45,000
Mining and quarrying	6,061
Industry	39,225
Electricity and water	5,078
Construction	6,000
Trade	44,000
Transportation and storage	32,000
Finance	11,370
Public administration, defense, and other services	211,734

Source: Jordanian Department of Statistics, *Statistical Yearbook* 1983.

class in income only. It does not have middle-class values or lifestyle. A mechanic might make $2,000 a month. "This puts him in the middle class, but he is not educated and does not care much about what the traditional middle class in Jordan is now interested in: more democracy, justice, an active parliament." His pleasures are different. "The best market for video tapes is not in the rich areas but the slums," he comments.

But not everyone in the slums is buying video tapes. Some, many in fact, remain poor. As this same observer says, "Three decades ago we had a balanced society. The poor were not very poor, the rich were not very rich. Now we have the rise of a very rich class that is evident, and there are those who, relatively speaking, are very poor. . . .The economic inequities," he concludes, "are the most likely cause of serious unrest if it should come."

Others make the same point. A prosperous, hustling young Jordanian- Palestinian businessman says he had not thought much about the problem until one day he was coming across the bridge from the West Bank. A Jordanian customs guard remarked with some heat that he could not afford even to be buried on Jebel Amman, let alone live there. Not long after that, the businessman recounted, a taxi driver turned on him with a retort that could only mean, "We'll get you rich people some day." It was evident that the businessman, while no doubt glad to be doing well, was dismayed to find himself regarded as a class enemy.

The poor have not been as badly off as they might have been had the boom brought with it the heated inflation that often accompanies sudden prosperity. At the height of the upward surge in 1979 and 1980, consumer prices increased by 14.3 percent and 11.0 percent, respectively, with some hardship to families on marginal incomes; but the increase was brought down to 7.7 percent in 1981, to 7.4 percent the next year, 5.0 percent in 1983 and 3.9 percent in 1984 primarily by government control of the money supply.

The Boom Levels Off

The remarkable upward trajectory of Jordan's economy has now been leveling off. Beginning about 1981, all of the kingdom's major sources of income were in some degree of trouble. GNP growth increased at the extraordinary rate of 17.1 percent in 1981, but slipped to 5.7 and 5.4 percent in 1982 and 1983, and to 4 percent in 1984. Nevertheless a growth rate of over 5 percent is considered good performance by world standards, and even 4 percent is respectable. Jordan thus still seems to be playing its economic cards well, though there may not be so many face cards and aces as there were for a while.

Jordan's basic problem has been a downturn in the economies of the Gulf states. The demand for oil and its price have both fallen sharply, and with them the incomes of those countries. A leading Jordanian economist and banker comments that the problem is as bad as it is not because of the drop in oil income alone, but because the Gulf economies were so mismanaged during the boom years. "Grotesque waste" occurred, he says, and mismanagement caused "huge declines in excess funds" during those years. As a result, the supply of jobs for foreign workers has shrunk. Remittances have leveled off, though for 1984 they appeared to turn up somewhat. It is doubly important for Jordan that they not suffer sharp declines. First, they are the most important single source of foreign exchange. And second, a decline would mean return of workers to Jordan, with the threat it poses of renewed unemployment and social tension.

Most observers believe that a plateau, or at worst a slight dip, has been reached in remittance payments. A prominent banker states that no more workers are going out and a limited number are coming back. Those who return bring their capital with them—though most do not have much capital—and at first this masks the fact that they are no longer sending back a salary. In time, he fears, this will show up as a loss.

How much of a problem this turns out to be will depend, of course, on the performance of the oil economy, and there is little Jordan can do to influence it. It appears, however, that Jordanian workers in the Gulf states are riding out the slump better than other foreigners, for the Jordanians are white collar employees, highly paid workers hired individually whose jobs are not so affected by the recession. They have taken over the traditional Egyptian role in education, and have moved into the media and advertising as well. Unskilled laborers, from other countries, have been hired in large blocs for specific projects, and they have been hard hit. In addition, the Arab Gulf states have been concerned about the social effects of hiring Asians in large numbers. They have been sending their Asian workers home and replacing them with Arabs. At one time, Arab workers were thought of as a political threat, but the Arab Gulf states are now more confident of their security forces and somewhat less sensitive on this score.

In Jordan's case, there is a further factor. Jordanian military relationships with some of the Gulf states, especially Saudi Arabia, have created bonds that inhibit any inclination to send Jordanian workers home.

If remittances have held up, the same has not been true of either subsidies from the Arab oil states or trade with Iraq. As cited earlier, the subsidies began to fall off soon after the 1978 Baghdad summit meeting that established them, even before the downturn in the oil economies. By 1984 the figure was well under half the $1.25 billion total agreed on at Baghdad.

The trade with Iraq fell off in 1983. The Iraqis' share in Jordanian exports dropped to 16.2 percent in that year (from 37.5 percent two years before), well below Saudi Arabia's share of 22 percent. In absolute terms, exports to Iraq fell from 66,579,811 JD in 1982 to 26,010,854 JD in the following year. The war with Iran, which had made Jordan so especially important to Iraq, was putting a heavy strain on the treasury in Baghdad, and the drop in oil revenues compounded Iraq's difficulties. Jordan found itself subsidizing Iraq, in effect, by supporting the manufacturing industries set up for the Iraqi trade. There is still talk of a pipeline to Aqaba but meanwhile oil is being trucked to the port. The year 1984 saw an upturn in Iraqi imports, which could well be short-lived. The first four months of 1985 again showed a drop. As one commentator put it, the Iraqis turn the tap off and on quite unpredictably.

At the same time, the world market for phosphate went through a deep trough. After several excellent years, the demand fell off beginning in 1981 and the price dropped as well. The market and price improved in 1984, bringing an export return more than a third higher than that of 1983.

With the precipitate decline of the Iraqi trade, and the weakening in the phosphate market, Jordan's export earnings fell from $752 million in 1982 to $580 million in 1983. In 1984, with the Iraqi import jump and the phosphate upturn, they rose again to about the 1982 levels. Imports were cut back slightly in 1983 and 1984 as well, but at about $2.5 billion remained several times the level of exports.

The deficit in the current accounts balance has steadily increased since 1980, when there was a rare surplus. Including the very negative import-export trade balance, the receipts and payments for services (including remittances coming in and going out), and transfer payments to Jordan such as Arab subsidies, the country spent $391 million more than it took in for 1983. In 1984, the gap was about $350 million. The deficit was covered primarily by borrowing and the drawing-down of Central Bank reserves.

The daily economic life of the kingdom has certainly been affected by the combination of shocks from abroad, but there have as yet been no serious dislocations. Unemployment has edged gradually upward to around 6 percent. Some workers have returned from the Gulf states, but there seems to have been no major influx. True, the days are gone when a worker in Jordan could look to the economic frontier of the Persian Gulf as a place to escape the confines of the local job market. Jordan must now absorb the labor supply as it becomes available, including the women who can be expected to enter the labor force in growing numbers. With an annual increase of 6 percent in the labor supply, experts fear Jordan cannot absorb more than half of the new workers each year. Even if the oil economies pick up in years to come, the nationals of the larger Gulf states will have become sufficiently educated and trained to take some of the jobs that might in earlier times have gone to foreigners.

To put itself in a better position to deal with a tightening job market the government has begun to clamp down on foreign labor. An amendment to the labor law prohibits the hiring of foreigners for administrative or clerical jobs and requires all expatriate workers to have permits. The Jordanian householder with an Asian servant or the commercial employer of Egyptian laborers may now find it harder to get or renew permits. Some foreign workers have left. The government itself is making do with fewer expatriate employees. Foreign crew members of the Royal Jordanian Airline, for example, are in some cases being replaced by Jordanians.

Business in the country is slow. A private businessman, asked about conditions, said the only company he could think of that was prospering was the government's Ministry of Supply. The ministry imports and markets certain key commodities as well as some that are controlled to limit competition for domestic producers. The businessman's remark was a barbed one. Private entrepreneurs are increasingly concerned about the ministry's muscling in on the country's commerce, in the main a preserve of private enterprise.

One hears rumors that a collapse threatens in house mortgages. Certainly building has fallen off sharply; some say it is worse than that. Land values have started to drop and the market value of many new houses is said to be below the level of the mortgages readily granted by banks in the heady boom days. Workers in the Gulf region, their earnings down and facing an uncertain future, are said to be trying to unload their properties. It seems unlikely that Jordan's carefully managed financial sector could not handle the problem, but the worries are symptomatic of a changed climate.

There is a turning inward for investment capital as the largesse from abroad shrinks. The expanded banking system, newly oriented toward investment activities, must now help offset the loss. The Central Bank has conducted a campaign to persuade an unaccustomed public to put its money to work, "to utilize the savings of the community rather than have them kept in the mattress," in the words of the Bank's Deputy Governor, Husayn S. al Kasim.

To the extent that foreign borrowing becomes necessary, Jordan's international credit is reasonably good. The borrowings that have been necessary to offset the current account deficit have still left modest debt levels for a country the size of Jordan. Moreover, most of the loans have been from foreign governments at concessionary interest rates rather than from commercial banks abroad (Table 4). Debt servicing is relatively low, a major plus in an era in which it has become an economic disaster for so many Third World countries.

Jordan seems thus far to be riding out the ebbing of the oil tide fairly well. If the oil market turns up or the Iraq-Iran war ends, the kingdom is well positioned to bounce back. There are still some clouds on the distant horizon, however, especially with the further softening of oil prices at the end of 1985 and early 1986. If more Jordanian workers return from the Gulf than is generally expected, unemployment could rise uncomfortably. If the Saudis continue to cut back on subsidy payments—the current arrangement is due to expire in 1988—the budget and balance-of-payments deficits could become more difficult to manage. More basically, a predominantly service-oriented economy is always more vulnerable to outside shocks, and the Middle East is a tough neighborhood.

Perhaps the blackest cloud of all, once again, arises from the Palestinian problem. If Israel pursues policies that generates large-scale refugee flight from the West Bank into Jordan, all the fine-tuned balancing would be overwhelmed.

Possibilities for Economic Independence

Jordan has evolved a generally effective mixture of laïssez-faire and government management. Most of the country's economic activity—agriculture, commerce, smaller-scale industry, banking—is free enterprise that thrives on a minimum of regulation and the entrepreneurial spirit, especially that of the Palestinians. The government owns or controls transportation, communications, electric power, and the large-scale (400 or more employees) manufacturing industries: phosphates, cement, and paper. It also controls the tourism industry. Smaller manufacturing enterprises may have some degree of government participation as well.

On this basis, the economy works probably better than most in the Third World. But there are still weaknesses and dependencies. Can these be eliminated or reduced? The consensus in the country seems to be a very qualified yes, at least so far as foreign aid is concerned. No country the size of Jordan, with its scarcity of resources, can become independent of the political and economic climate in the outside world, especially its own region. The very process of gaining more economic independence through development of its only real potential—its service function—ironically enough increases its dependence on the region for which, in the last analysis, it performs its services.

Tourism, banking, education, and intertrade are four service industries often spoken of as offering possibilities for expansion. Exploiting their potential will require more than investment and other economic inputs, however. Some Jordanians speak of a provincial state of mind at official levels that inhibits development beyond a certain point. An exasperated businessman exclaims, "We are the only country that builds hotels and discourages tourism." A leading entrepreneur in the hotel business feels that the government is fearful of a larger tourist trade, which it sees as raising troublesome internal security problems or friction with the Muslim fanatics. A leading banker complains that there is no way Jordan can inherit any of the international banking that has fled Beirut as a result of the Lebanese civil war. The foreign banks have gone to Bahrain instead. The Jordanian infrastructure of communications, international schools, and transportation in and out of the country is not up to it, he argues. In addition, he contends, the Jordanian banking laws are not hospitable. Others comment, too, that the government appears to want the Jordanization of banks, which are required (with exceptions for some foreign banks) to invest 15 percent of their deposits in local enterprises. Insurance companies are also subject to the requirement that they deposit part of their accounts in Jordan and acquire shares in local development projects.

There are, of course, risks and other costs to opening up the country to foreign enterprise and creating conditions that appeal to and attract foreign consumers and providers of services. In banking, for example, foreign banks operating without close national supervision can transfer their capital out of the country in times of crisis—times when this is most disadvantageous for the host state. Insurance companies can and do invest their deposits abroad, not benefiting the local economy and risking an inability to cover large claims that may arise.

It is understandable that Jordan should feel the need to maintain a level of control that inhibits maximum expansion of its economic potential in a number of areas. The kingdom has survived through prudent management in the political, social and economic sectors. In economic expansion, a gradual evolution under careful control is probably the only prudent course. So many and such major aspects of the kingdom's international environment are out of its control and quite unpredictable that a tendency to keep critical aspects of its domestic life on a fairly tight rein would seem justified. Over the long term it would be highly desirable to reduce Jordanian dependence on foreign subsidies. But the life and death problems always seem to lie in the shorter term, and they take precedence.

The West Bank Relationship

Political involvement with the Israeli-occupied West Bank will be dealt with later. Since the interrelationships among the Jordanian, Israeli, and West Bank economies are significant in thinking about political futures, they deserve some attention at this point. The key question is whether the West Bank is so economically tied to Israel that any thought of its returning to a relationship with Jordan is unrealistic.

The economic has been shaped by the military and political. Between 1948 and 1967 the West Bank belonged to Jordan, and the ties were all with Amman. Few led across the armistice lines into Israel. After the 1967 war a much more complex situation developed. Israel linked the West Bank more and more to its own economy but permitted a high degree of permeability to continue between the territory and Jordan.

Under Jordanian rule ("during Jordan," as the West Bank man-in-the- street is prone to say) the West Bank was something of a stepchild of Amman. Agriculture remained largely undeveloped. The industrial sector saw little investment, the government authorizing no investment for more than 10,000 JD—about $28,000—in the whole period. The East Bank was given preference in all development plans, with government investment in irrigation, land reclamation, electricity, transport, and communications directed primarily to the East Bank.

Having started in 1948 considerably behind the West Bank, by 1967 the East Bank had 80 percent of the country's industry (in terms of value added), grew 80 percent of the wheat crop, and produced 80 percent of the principal agricultural export crop, tomatoes.

The West Bankers complain bitterly about Amman's treatment, but they themselves have also shown a distinct preference for investing on the East Bank, then and now. The political half-light in which the West Bank has existed since 1948 has not encouraged long-term investment by anyone.

Since 1967 the West Bank has become increasingly integrated with the Israeli economy, essentially for two reasons: the natural dynamics of the geographical and political situation, and Israeli design. Jordanian policies toward the territory have exacerbated this evolution.

One of the earliest, and certainly the most dramatic, forms of integration was the movement of tens of thousands of West Bank Arabs into the Israeli job market. In the early 1970s the Israeli economy was prosperous and growing rapidly. By 1971 a third of West Bank workers were employed in Israel, and endemic unemployment and underemployment in the West Bank had been virtually eliminated. West Bank agriculture was left in the hands of the women and children while the men went off to earn salaries double what was being paid in Jordan. Some farms went out of production, and others turned to producing for home consumption only. Complaints about how hard it was to find hands to harvest the important olive crop were heard on every side.

The Israeli economy turned down in 1973, and a large number of the West Bankers were thrown out of work. Many swung with the changing tide and went to work in Jordan, whose economy was expanding. A warming effect on Jordanian-West Bank relations resulted at the time. Nevertheless, West Bankers, together with residents of the Gaza Strip, have continued to supply about 8 percent of the Israeli labor force.

The West Bank's trade pattern has been another clear indication of rapidly developing ties with Israel. Almost 90 percent of imports are from or through Israel; only a trickle of imports comes from Jordan. Sixty percent of exports go to Israel. Exports to Jordan have of course fallen sharply since 1967 but are still substantial. They are roughly two-thirds agricultural, as is evident to any traveler from the long lines of trucks, loaded with tomatoes and other vegetables and fruits, waiting at the Israeli processing point by the bridge across the Jordan River.

Trade with Israel, both in and out, is largely industrial despite the relatively small role the industrial sector plays in the West Bank economy (6 to 8 percent of GNP). One explanation on the export side is that a substantial portion of the West Bank's workshop industry serves as sub-contractor to Israeli contractors. As for imports, the West Bank is a protected market for Israeli products. Goods from places other than Israel can be imported only with Israeli approval and only with payment of the Israeli import tax. Israeli products are in some cases priced even lower than West Bank equivalents, due to lower production costs and heavy subsidies in Israel. The West Bank market is of great value to Israel, taking at least a quarter of Israel's total exports.

West Bank farmers have been encouraged to grow crops that fit into the Israeli economic pattern. Shortly after 1967, for example, they were urged to switch from foods of high water content such as watermelons—intended for Arab markets to the east—to leguminous crops that, in the absence of other markets, could be preserved and marketed by the Israeli Agricultural Export Company.

In the last few years some West Bank farmers have planted crops they hoped would help them hold onto their land. With more and more land being taken by Israeli settlements, they have turned to crops that are a year-round presence, such as olive trees and grape vines, in the belief that land is less likely to be seized if something is visibly growing on it. The Mennonite Central Committee, a voluntary assistance agency, distributed 228,000 olive seedlings in one five-year period.

In nineteen years of occupation, the West Bank has been increasingly tied into the Israeli road and utility infrastructure. Road-building has been extensive but has been dedicated to linking Israeli settlements on the West Bank with each other and with Israel. A network along the heights above the Jordan valley has obvious military purposes. Electric power capacity has been a contentious issue. As West Bank communities have come to need more power, they have applied to the Israeli authorities for permission to import generators. Most of the applications have been rejected, and in some cases the towns have been tied into the Israeli electrical grids. West Bank communities have had the same experience in meeting increased water needs. Applications for new wells have been turned down, and the towns have been tied into the Israeli system where that is available, as in the case of Ramallah, near Jerusalem.

In the supply of money and banking facilities, there has been more of a standoff between Israeli and Jordanian linkage. Arab banks were closed after the 1967 war. When given the green light by Israel to open some months later, none did. They are still closed. They would have had to operate within the Israeli banking system under the supervision of Israeli authorities, and neither the banks themselves nor the Jordanian government was prepared to accept that. Branches of Israeli banks did open on the West Bank; twenty-eight are now operation but are little used. The public prefers the relatively firm Jordanian dinar to the extremely weak and fluctuating Israeli currency. The dinar is legal tender on the West Bank, and residents of the area have access to banks in Jordan. Israeli banks do not pay interest on dinar accounts and in fact charge a commission for them.

West Bank money changers have evolved into a kind of surrogate banking system. They transfer money to the Amman banks for long-term deposits and handle current cash transactions themselves. There is a very substantial flow of currency back and forth across the Jordan River. A 1979 survey estimated that in one month (December) roughly a billion Israeli pounds in dollars and dinars entered the West Bank from Jordan and about half as much went the other way. Since there is no banking system through which transfers can be made, payments for imports and exports, Jordanian salaries still paid to certain employees on the West Bank, and other transactions must be made in cash carried across the river.

The establishment of an Arab bank on the West Bank has been the subject of active negotiation since 1984. Israeli authorities have agreed in principle to some form of hybrid institution, but Amman has been very reserved. Jordanians are unwilling that any type of regulation be exercised by the Israelis. The project is also apparently caught in bureaucratic cross-fire in Amman, and Jordanian banks once operative on the West Bank are said to have their own problems with it. The suspicions and hostilities, and the multitude of conflicting self-interests that have evolved, seem likely to frustrate the scheme until the basic political pattern is changed.

In this case Jordanian policy has shown the same narrow and self-defeating tendency that has hampered it in other ways from maintaining its relationship with the West Bank. Jordan will admit West Bank industrial imports only from enterprises using raw materials imported from Jordan. Trade ties between Jordan and the West Bank have inevitably been limited by such regulations, not to mention the impediments imposed by the required paperwork and security checking at the border.

As to the feasibility of shifting West Bank ties back to Jordan in some form, the short answer is that the economic follows the military and political, as it did in 1967. But such an answer, while correct, obscures the difficulties, which would in some ways be greater than they were in 1967. The West Bank economy is still so relatively unde- veloped—little investment having been made in it under either Jorda- nian or Israeli rule—that trade and production patterns could be shifted again without prolonged trauma. But the physical infrastruc- ture—road patterns, electricity and water connections, land owner- ship and use by Israeli settlements—would be more of a problem. Indeed, the question of land use and ownership would be one of the more sensitive issues in any peace negotiation.

Employment of West Bank and Gaza residents in Israel would also pose problems. Both Arabs and Israel would face serious short-run dislocations if this employment relationship were broken off by a peace settlement. Jordan's capacity to absorb West Bank and Gaza workers no longer able to seek jobs in Israel—at least until the economic devel- opment of the territories could be stimulated enough to create jobs there—would depend on the state of its economy at the time. In to- day's languishing economy it would be a problem, although Palestin- ian workers could presumably replace to some extent the foreign work- ers still employed in Jordan.

The difficulties in disentangling Israel and the occupied territories suggest that both would benefit by a peace settlement that avoided sealing off the two economies from one another. The West Bank has ties to both Jordan and Israel now; it would be anomalous if in a state of peace it becomes more isolated.

The stability of Jordan's internal and political relationships is un- usually sensitive to the state of the economy. Internal strains have been reduced by the past economic expansion and, by the same token, could be exacerbated if the downturn becomes more serious. In the slow- down since 1981 the positive effects of an expanding economy have largely been lost, but the situation has not become bad enough to produce real strains. An uneasy balance is being maintained. In 1984, income from remittances and exports increased and imports were cut, but the benefits were offset by a continued drop in subsidies from the Gulf states. Central Bank reserves had to be used to cover the remain- ing payments gap. State-sponsored economic development is having to be cut back to keep government budgets in line.

Prolongation of the slump, even if the balance-of-payments situa- tion became no worse, would bring some problems. Borrowing to fill the payments gap when bank reserves were insufficient would run up the country's debt. With the economy developing so slowly, it would be able to absorb only about half the Jordanians coming onto the job market each year. Competition for scarce jobs would heighten social tensions and exacerbate the rich-poor gap.

Should the economic situation worsen markedly for Jordan, with balance-of-payments figures turning more negative and Jordanian workers returning in larger numbers from the Gulf region to look for jobs at home, more serious problems would arise. Unemployment would grow even over the short term; living standards could be affected by import cuts; the government would have increasing trouble paying army and civil service salaries; and economic development would dry up. The social and political fabric would begin to fray.

Which way things go depends on events and decisions beyond Jordan's borders that no one can predict with any confidence. The boom seems clearly to be over for some time to come, but there has been hope that the situation would stabilize at a lower, and tolerable, level of growth. The move in late 1985 by the Organization of Oil Producing Countries (OPEC) to allow oil prices to drop further makes such a projection seem optimistic, however. An important, only partly economic, factor is the decision the Gulf state governments will make each year about subsidy payments to Jordan. Without these subsidies, or something to take their place, the payment gap would more than double even if everything else held firm. The King has to consider this as he plots a course for peace negotiations.

Whatever the future holds, Jordan is a country that has been much changed by the years of rapid economic growth. While it is still dependent on external assistance in some form, and probably will remain so, it is better able than it once was to deal with shocks and strains. It has also developed a distinctive economic character, an amalgam of active free enterprise and relatively effective government management of the more sensitive and vulnerable areas of economic life. In the process the country has achieved a certain economic solidity that contributes to its sense of national identity and its durability as a state.

6

Jordan's Future and the Palestinian Question

With the approach of the Israeli elections scheduled for July 23, 1984, there was hope in Amman that their results might make the Palestinian problem more manageable, that a serious effort to settle it might even become possible. The Israeli government had been dominated for seven years by the Likud bloc of right-wing parties headed for most of the period by Prime Minister Menachem Begin. Under his leadership Israel had made abundantly clear that it had no intention of giving up any of the West Bank, a position that effectively ruled out a solution of the Palestinian problem acceptable to the Arabs. Now, in the spring and early summer of 1984, Israeli polls showed Likud far enough behind the Israeli Labor Party that it seemed the seven-year rule of the right wing was coming to an end.

To be sure, the Labor Party, which would form the next government if the polls were borne out, had not been a soft touch on the Palestinian problem either. It had not been prepared to negotiate away enough of the West Bank to tempt King Hussein into a negotiation. One of its Prime Ministers, Golda Meir, had scoffed that there were no such people as the Palestinians. But Labor Party leaders were not ideologues. They did not feel themselves bound by sacred biblical injunction or historical imperative to retain every inch of the West Bank for Israel. Indeed, General Yitzak Rabin, for several years a Labor Prime Minister, had once been quoted as saying he regarded the Bible as a book of ethics, not of geography.

In Amman, Labor seemed a familiar and, after Likud, a more benign face of Israel. It was possible that one could, with a Labor

117

government, get some diplomatic movement underway. At the very least, the threat that had cast such a shadow across the Jordan River would be considerably reduced.

Hopes for a clear Labor victory were dashed in Amman as in many other capitals by the results of the July 23 elections. Likud, to be sure, lost ground, but so did Labor. The smaller parties of the extreme right and left gained what the two giants had lost. Even though Labor emerged with 44 seats in the Knesset (Israel's parliament) to Likud's 41, it was not at all certain that it could form a government. Even if it did, would it have the clear dominance that would be necessary if it were to lead Israel down a path toward a Palestinian solution that would be bitterly resisted by powerful forces within the country?

Jordanians watched with little optimism the prolonged horse-trading in Israel over the setting up of a new government. The somewhat surprising deal that eventually emerged was no cause for rejoicing, but it contained both an opening and a threat that led King Hussein and at least some of his advisers to decide that they should act. Labor was to head a joint Labor-Likud government for half the four-year period until the next elections. That was the opening. The threat was that at the end of two years Likud would take over for the rest of the period. The Jordanians saw a slightly open window of two years.

As the King and his advisers assessed Jordan's situation in the wake of the Israeli election and considered what course of action to take, they did so against a complex but familiar background of history and politics. While Jordan has developed into a rounded state with a variety of interests and relationships, as is clear from the preceding chapters the Palestinian question continues to dominate its concerns. King Hussein, in a November 2, 1985, speech opening a new session of Parliament, said that "the Palestinian problem . . . has been and will continue to be our main preoccupation."

Moves on that chessboard bring into play Jordan's most vital interests, national and dynastic Hashemite goals, and the constraints imposed by Jordan's position in the region. They are shaped by the nature of the Palestinian question as it has evolved, by Jordan's relationships with the West Bank and with the PLO, by judgments about Israeli intentions, and by the pattern of managing the problem that has developed over the years.

Careful attention had to be given by the Jordanian leadership to recent moves by all key players. Finally, a number of difficult questions inevitably arose that, articulated or not, were central: Is the *modus vivendi* that has evolved among Jordan, the West Bank, and Israel perhaps the real "solution" to the problem in this imperfect world? Are the dangers of high-profile peace diplomacy too great for Jordan, especially given the odds against success? Or, on the contrary, is peace diplomacy an essential component of the *modus vivendi* itself and necessary as well to maintain Jordan's position in the world, especially its relationship with the United States? What is the balance of risks?

Aims and Constraints

The integrity of the state and its security from foreign and domestic threats, the survival of the monarchy as an institution, and the security of the King's hold on his throne are related imperatives that head the list of policy goals in Amman. They are not taken for granted. Jordan and its monarchy have lived too close to the edge for that.

Beyond the country's borders, Jordan's leadership wants the cultivation of a moderate political environment in the region that reduces security strains; enough regional friends to balance the adversaries; and the steady support of the United States, politically, economically, and as a supplier of military equipment. At home, the leadership looks for stability; continued loyalty to the monarchy—or at least acquiescence in it—by the key elements in the population; the continued welding together of a cohesive national society that includes the Palestinians; and an even keel, with some development, in the economy.

For the King there is another goal inherited from his Hashemite forebears: the drive to play a larger role, to do more than manage the affairs of a small and dependent state. It is not only a matter of governing more—and more consequential—territory or regaining Jerusalem. Even the diplomatic game of making peace—conferring in Washington and in European and Arab capitals, commanding headlines, being a center of purposeful international activity—is a kind of larger stage in itself.

Except for the last, these are not exceptional goals for a state. A look at the constraints under which the kingdom operates, however, reveals how calculatingly policy must be managed to secure them. But more than calculation is needed. In the shifting sands of the Middle East, especially for the monarch of a small and weak state, staying on top requires constant movement, nimbleness, and not a little daring.

From the time he took over the throne, Hussein's freedom of action has been limited by Jordan's situation in a number of ways. Externally, the vulnerability and dependence of the kingdom place serious constraints on policy. Domestically, the population split between a Palestinian majority and a large East Banker minority on which the King depends ultimately for his support makes for a complex set of pressures and counterpressures.

The most basic weakness is economic. Jordan must have substantial subsidies from some outside source to avoid wrenching and destabilizing dislocations. Without them it cannot support the army, pay government salaries, and maintain anything like the level of imports the country has grown accustomed to. Harsh economies would strike at the survivability of the monarchy. The army and much of the bureaucracy are instruments of power and at the same time provide major subsidies, in effect, to the East Bank population that disproportionately composes them. Continuing imports, and a reasonable level of economic activity generally, satisfy an increasingly consumption-oriented middle class consisting disproportionately of Palestinians, whose economic satisfaction is an important factor in their acceptance of Hashemite rule. In the past, Jordan's subsidies have been cut off when the King departed from the Arab mainstream on Palestinian issues.

Jordan's vulnerability to political isolation, subversion and outright military aggression is also never far from the thoughts of the leadership in Amman. Borders and airspace can be closed, trade cut off, officials assassinated, the kingdom branded an outcast in the Arab World. It has all happened.

Jordan is, of course, not without strengths of its own. Its position as a buffer among hostile states is the most obvious. The Israelis, the Syrians, and the Saudis particularly have a stake in Jordan's remaining independent rather than coming under the influence of a hostile neighbor. As a moderate, Western-oriented state, Jordan has been considered an asset by Britain and the United States; it has, in effect, provided services they have been willing to pay for.

The United States has been especially important. American financial support paid directly into the budget, together with smaller amounts supplied covertly to Hussein, largely made it possible for the King to hold things together from the time the British faded from the scene in 1956 until the Arab oil states began picking up the tab after the 1967 war, but more generously after Camp David in 1978. Major political efforts by the United States helped turn back or deter Syrian attacks in 1970 and 1980. American weapons, despite the sometimes extreme difficulty of obtaining them, contribute critically to Jordan's military capability.

Among Arab states, Saudi Arabia has been the most important to Jordan economically. Jordan, in turn, plays a unique role in the Saudis' scheme of things. It was not always so. Having chased the Hashemites out of the Hejaz in the early 1920s and having been frustrated in their raids on Jordan in 1922 and 1924, the Saudis persisted in their hostility until the Hashemite monarchy of Feisal was overthrown in Iraq in 1958. Apparently realizing at that point that conservative monarchies were an endangered species, they swung to a more supportive attitude toward Hussein which, with some lapses, has generally prevailed since. They have, of course, other reasons to value Jordan's presence as buffer and shield.

The Saudis are difficult allies and patrons, however. One leading Jordanian calls them the curse of Arab politics. Rich and weak, they protect themselves in a dangerous world by avoiding actions or policies that could bring them into opposition to states or forces they fear could hurt them. Many would say that they simply avoid actions or policies—period. The Saudis prefer an atmosphere of consensus and will seldom buck the tide or take a stand, even on behalf of the Jordanians.

Jordan also derives strength and maneuvering room from the cleavages and rivalries among its neighbors. Syria and Egypt have frequently been rivals for regional dominance, and Syria and Iraq have been adversaries under their competing Baath party regimes. Less directly, the global U.S.-Soviet competition has invested Jordan with a special value in American eyes.

The presence of a Palestinian majority in the population influences and constrains Jordanian policy more than any other domestic factor. It is not so much that Palestinian-Jordanians as a group press for particular policies, although they did so vociferously in the 1940s and 1950s. They have in recent years been remarkably quiescent politically. The King is aware, however, that substantial numbers of this majority of his subjects withhold a full commitment to his rule. He knows, too, that the dynamics of the larger Palestinian question—volatile and violent as it is—with all of its regional manifestations, inevitably has an impact on the Palestinian majority.

In these circumstances Hussein is especially reliant on the East Banker minority. East Bankers have their own important sensitivities, however, especially when it comes to Jordan's relationship with the Palestinian problem. Although these are not monolithic views, they are strongly held in some circles, such as the military leadership, and they must be catered to. Hussein has been careful over the years to avoid identifying himself with the most narrow and conservative elements among the East Bankers; he has understood the need to win the cooperation and at least acquiescent loyalty of the Palestinians. But he can only go so far without jeopardizing his bedrock East Bank base of support.

The Palestinian Question

At the heart of the Palestinian question, for Jordan, has been the interlaced relationship among Jordan, the West Bank, and Israel. The impact of the wider Palestinian diaspora, through the Palestinian national movement and particularly the PLO, has also been important, especially since 1967.

The problem, from Jordan's point of view, has undergone a significant transformation since 1970. In the wake of the 1967 war the U.N. Security Council adopted Resolution 242 that was intended to and did serve as a set of principles for solving the Arab-Israeli conflict. The heart of the resolution is a deal in which the Arabs would give up their struggle against Israel—terminate "all claims and states of belligerency"—in exchange for "withdrawal of Israeli armed forces from territories occupied as a result of the 1967 conflict." The resolution reflected a common assumption of the time that occupied territories would be returned to the authorities that had controlled them before the war. In the case of the West Bank this was Jordan. The Palestinians were referred to in the resolution only as refugees.

The PLO changed all that. Through its stepped-up raids against Israel (who else was carrying the fight to Israel?); through the notoriety resulting from its terrorism; through the recruitment, training and arming of large militias; through some strong-arm tactics among Palestinians and with Arab governments. Most important, the PLO became the only game in town in promoting the interest of the Palestinians before any other priority, and it achieved widespread influence among Palestinians and Arabs generally, including Arab governments. It pronounced, for the first time, policy for Palestinians. To be sure, the policy was a little rubbery at any given time and went through gradual evolution, but the ideas of self-determination for Palestinians and a Palestinian state were central to it.

The transformation of the problem was formalized by the Rabat summit meeting of Arab League heads of state in 1974, designating the PLO as the sole legitimate representative of the Palestinians. Two things were revolutionary about this. First, the Palestinians were now, in effect, to represent themselves; and second, the Palestinians became collectively a necessary player in any negotiated settlement.

Another change in Jordan's relationship to the Palestinian question after 1967 concerned the Gaza Strip. This hot, flat, sandy bit of territory along the southern coast of Palestine was held by Egyptian forces in the 1948 war and occupied by Egypt thereafter. It was kept at a distance politically by the Egyptian government, however, and its people were not offered Egyptian citizenship. It had little or no connection with Jordan; the Jordanian citizenship that was extended to Palestinians on the West Bank, incorporated into Jordan, was not available in the Gaza Strip.

Israel seized and occupied the Gaza Strip in the 1967 war. In the light of U.N. Resolution 242 there was a supposition that Egypt remained the Arab government entrusted with the territory. But as the Palestinian national movement asserted itself, Gaza began to be thought of, together with the West Bank, as the area that would constitute a Palestinian entity in any peace settlement.

King Hussein, in his United Arab Kingdom plan of 1972, included Gaza as part of the Palestinian entity that would, with Jordan, compose the federated kingdom. The subsequent Camp David agreement between Egypt and Israel, in its provisions for Palestinian autonomy, included Gaza with the West Bank as the area in question. In general, though, the Strip existed in a kind of limbo politically, with almost all the focus of discussion on the West Bank as a residual Palestinian homeland.

Although it has been so often disregarded, the Gaza Strip is by no means unimportant. It has roughly 500,000 inhabitants, compared with the 750,000 West Bankers, packed into an area far smaller than the West Bank. Four-fifths of the population are refugees, contrasted with a quarter of West Bankers. Palestinian militancy flourished in the far poorer conditions of Gaza at a time when it was less evident in the West Bank. But there has been less organized political activity, given the near absence—in the heavily refugee camp population—of the social and political infrastructure and the large educated professional class that exist on the West Bank.

With the evolution of the Palestinian problem since 1967, the West Bank has become an important, if somewhat reluctant, player in its own right. It is the largest intact indigenous society of Palestinians and thus has been the centerpiece of demands from many Arab quarters for an independent Palestinian state. The United States and the Israeli

Labor Party have entertained the hope in recent years that West Bankers would put themselves forward in place of the PLO as the Palestinian representatives with Jordan in any peace negotiation. Jordan, for its part, has hoped that the West Bankers would induce the PLO to adopt more pragmatic policies toward peace negotiations. The relationship between Jordan and the West Bank, never easy, has become more complex on both sides.

For all its 19 years of rule from Amman, the West Bank was not significantly Jordanianized when the Israelis took over in 1967. West Bankers thought of the Jordanians more as occupiers than as fellow countrymen, and for the most part they disliked and feared the Arab Legion that enforced the occupation. They were very conscious of the fact that all the district governors in the territory except one—Anwar Khatib in Jerusalem—were Jordanians, not West Bankers.

The Amman-West Bank relationship remained complicated even after the territory came under Israeli occupation in 1967. The population, much as it disliked Israel and wanted to be rid of the occupation, did not yearn for the return of the Arab Legion. The estrangement was increased by the crushing of the PLO militias in 1970–71, which caused great bitterness on the West Bank. On the other hand, West Bankers have remained Jordanian citizens, have used Jordanian currency as much as they can, have traded and traveled back and forth across the Jordan River. Many of their children have attended the universities in Jordan. Some Jordanian laws have continued to apply on the West Bank.

From 1974 on, Jordan began to reduce its presence and its influence on the West Bank as a reaction to the Rabat summit decision on Palestinian representation. By the 1980s Jordanian influence had been considerably cut back. It was said by West Bankers that if you offended the Jews, you were punished by the occupation forces; if you offended Syria or the PLO, someone would burn your car; but you could say whatever you wanted about Jordan and nothing would happen to you. Moderates such as Mayor Elias Freij of Bethlehem criticized Jordan for having run down its political capital, and alluded to Amman's unwillingness to provide any financing except through the Joint Committee with the PLO as part of the problem.

If West Bankers were not anxious to return to Jordanian control, they wanted with increasing urgency to be out from under Israeli control. They felt, moreover, that time was running out on any chance of this happening. The Israeli government already had more than half the land on the West Bank by 1984. There were more than 40,000

Israelis living in 128 settlements throughout the territory. Most of them were in suburban settlements around Jerusalem, but religious-nationalist zealots and the Likud government had seen to it that Israelis had struck roots throughout the area. Their presence, made doubly oppressive to the Arab population by the armed and militant settlers of the religious right wing who were moved into many settlements, added to the sense of desperation West Bankers felt about their lives.

Arabs on the West Bank were as familiar as Jordanians with the proposals of some Israelis to force them out and to make Jordan the Palestinian state. For some, this increased their determination to stay, not to make it easy for Israel by abandoning their homes. For others, however, it made staying and enduring seem pointless. Emigration had long been built into West Bank life—to the United States and Latin America, and more recently to the Gulf states. There was a steady seepage to Jordan as well. To keep the West Bank population from draining into Jordan, the Jordanian government cut this seepage off in 1983 by prohibiting entry to West Bankers who had no permit to return to the West Bank and by limiting the stay of West Bankers in Jordan to thirty days. Jordanian-West Bank relations were not improved by this move, which brought an outcry from Palestinians.

For all the urgency and the growing despair about the future, however, leading figures on the West Bank remained firm that:

- The West Bankers would not undertake to negotiate with Israel about the future status of the territory.

- While Jordan would probably have to take the initiative in getting negotiations underway, and should do so without delay, Jordan could not negotiate for them unless the PLO agreed that it should.

- Short of such agreement by the PLO, unlikely to be forthcoming, the PLO itself was their legitimate representative. The PLO, however, should move promptly toward negotiations.

To some extent this loyalty to the PLO reflected a concern for their own personal well-being, for the PLO could and did punish too much independence of mind by prominent West Bankers. But more important, it sprang from an appreciation of their own weak position in dealing with the Israeli occupying power as well as the fact that they could represent only the West Bank, not all the Palestinians. As a prominent, pro-Jordanian notable put it, "We can speak only for the

West Bank, but that doesn't solve the Palestinian problem We can't speak for the people from Jaffa [former Arab city in pre-1967 Israel.]"

Their unwillingness to give Jordan the mandate to represent them reflected in part their distrust of Amman and their fear that any agreement reached on this basis would put them back in Jordan's pocket. It also reflected, as a leading Palestinian adviser in Amman expressed it, the belief of at least some West Bankers that while Jordan could represent their *interests*, it could not represent their *national aspirations*.

Looking to the PLO and Jordan took pressure off West Bank leaders but left them, as always, frustratingly dependent on others to solve their problems. In early 1984, therefore, a group of eighty prominent West Bankers representing a cross-section of the population (eight mayors, a number of lawyers, businessmen, etc.) addressed a written statement to Arafat and the King urging them to get on with a solution to the problem.

The PLO, Jordan and Peace Diplomacy

Jordan's relations with the PLO hit bottom after the Palestinian militias were driven from the country in 1971. In terms of peace diplomacy, however, the basic nature of the relationship remained unchanged at that point. Jordan continued to see itself as the logical representative of Palestinian interests in any peace settlement. The King's unilateral action in putting forward the United Arab Kingdom plan in 1972 was a reflection of this assumption.

After the 1974 Rabat summit, it was clear to Jordanians that the relationship had changed. They could no longer act in the diplomatic arena on the Palestinian question—if they did so at all—without a legitimate Palestinian partner or an explicit mandate from a legitimate Palestinian leadership. In practical terms that meant the PLO. From then on, the vexed question of which Palestinians should represent the Palestinian people as a whole became a familiar feature of peace diplomacy.

The issue next presented itself in the unsuccessful U.S. effort in the fall of 1977 to arrange for the reconvening of the Geneva Conference on an Arab-Israeli peace settlement, originally set up after the 1973 war. Two variations were considered for Palestinian representation: Palestinian members of a Jordanian delegation, or Palestinian members of a single Arab delegation representing all the Arab governments involved. Of the two, Hussein preferred the all-Arab delegation. The Israelis made clear that, however it was done, Palestinians who participated could not be readily identifiable as PLO representatives.

Egyptian President Anwar Sadat's stunning diplomatic stroke of visiting Jerusalem effectively ended the Geneva Conference effort and led, in time, to Camp David in September 1978. The two agreements that emerged from this U.S.-Egyptian-Israeli summit conference took Egypt out of the Arab-Israeli struggle and established a three-stage process for negotiating the future of the West Bank and Gaza. Jordan was to be invited to participate in this process.

In the negotiations provided for in the agreement looking toward the establishment of a self-governing authority in the West Bank and Gaza, the Egyptian and Jordanian delegations could include "Palestinians from the West Bank and Gaza or other Palestinians as mutually agreed." Israel, it could be assumed, would not agree to PLO participants. In subsequent negotiations to determine the final status of the West Bank and Gaza, and to draw up an Israeli-Jordanian peace treaty, the Palestinians to participate were explicitly designated as "elected representatives of the inhabitants of the West Bank and Gaza."

This one of the two Camp David agreements was in effect stillborn. Jordan refused to participate in the process, and the Palestinians rejected it, as did most of the Arab World. The Israelis were making it clear that any "autonomy" would be minimal and that, whatever the final status of the West Bank and Gaza was to be, Israel would retain sovereignty over them. Meanwhile there would be no halt to the establishment of Israeli settlements in the West Bank. There was not much in this to tempt Palestinians or Jordanians, especially given their intense distrust of Israel's Likud government. In any case, the outcome would at best not be a solution to the entire Palestinian problem.

Even leaving these objections aside, Hussein had no wish to join Sadat as an Arab pariah for negotiating separate deals with Israel. He also deeply resented being handed a script he was supposed to follow but in the preparation of which he had no role.

The next major move in peace diplomacy was President Ronald Reagan's Middle East initiative of September 1, 1982. September 1 was the day the last of the PLO militiamen withdrew from Beirut under pressure from invading Israeli forces. Reagan, in a public address that drew attention back to the basic Palestinian problem, proposed a negotiating process that would lead to self-government of the West Bank and Gaza "in association with Jordan." The first phase of the process would be a five-year transitional period of local self-rule in the territories—a concept derived from the Camp David accords—to be followed by negotiation of the final status. The proposal called, in effect, for a freeze on Israeli settlements during this period.

Hussein reacted positively to the American initiative. He realized, however, that given the Rabat decision, the Arafat PLO leadership would have to be persuaded to participate before the process could take on reality.

By that time, Arafat was in somewhat reduced circumstances. He had been reluctantly received in Tunis after being driven out of Beirut. His militia was scattered; 500 of his men were in Tunis with him, and the rest were in Syria or in Syrian-controlled parts of Lebanon. He still ran an intact PLO political organization, however, and his political position seemed not too badly damaged on the whole.

The Jordanians negotiated with him for five months to get PLO agreement to work jointly for a confederal Jordanian-Palestinian solution, along the lines suggested by Reagan. Arafat no doubt encountered opposition to the proposal within the PLO leadership and from Syria. He presumably also came under Soviet pressure to turn it down. During a visit to Moscow in late 1982, Hussein was told by then Soviet Premier Yuri Andropov that the Soviets would do all they could to frustrate his efforts with the PLO.

In the end, the Jordanians failed. Arafat flew off from Amman with a draft agreement in his pocket for PLO-Jordanian cooperation, saying he would discuss it with PLO leaders. Five days later he sent back a new set of ideas that, in effect, scuttled the effort. The Jordanians threw in the towel. In a discouraged public statement of April 10, 1983, they left it to the PLO and the Palestinian people to find their own salvation.

A year and half later, following the Israeli elections, as the King and his advisers reconsidered the possibility of helping the PLO and the Palestinian people find their salvation, Arafat's position had worsened markedly. A Syrian-supported revolt in the ranks of his own faction of the PLO, Fatah, culminating in pitched battles in Tripoli, Lebanon, left him much weakened. His principal constituency had been reduced to the population of the West Bank and Gaza. His international image was tarnished. He needed a new course of action that would give him the opportunity to regain some control over events.

The decision that had to be made in the palace in Amman in the fall and winter of 1984–85 brought together all these components of Jordan's situation, distilled into a calculus of risks and advantages. At one level the issue could be simply put. Were the risks of letting the Palestinian problem drift greater than the risks to all of Jordan's relationships in the region of attempting to negotiate a peace settlement?

Both sets of risks were and are very real and generally well understood. The unresolved Palestinian problem is, in the first instance, simply a continuing uncertainty. In the best of circumstances the distinction between Palestinians and East Bankers might well fade gradually. But in the more likely event of recurring tension and conflict affecting the regional Palestinian question, the internal Jordanian split could become worse. Tensions springing from this split will remain, hanging over the society and government and complicating efforts to cope with the economic and political problems that come along. Unemployment, for example, will not be solely an economic question but an occasion for pressure on this delicate relationship.

The PLO, or something like it, will continue to operate. Inevitably it will be another claim on the loyalty of Palestinian-Jordanians. No one expects another 1970 civil war. But even the political presence of a Palestinian national representation is yet another front for the Jordanian government to cover in its complex game of staying alive in the turbulence of the Middle East. We have seen how friction between the government and the PLO can increase tensions between East Bankers and Palestinians.

Managing the succession will be chancier thing if the Palestinian issue still hangs over the country when Hussein goes. There will almost certainly be those, in and out of Jordan, who will see that as an opportunity to turn the country over to the Palestinian majority if the national status of that majority has not been resolved.

The danger, on the other hand, of venturing out essentially alone to try for a solution is even more clear. The Hashemites bear the scars of swimming against the Arab current on the Palestinian question. A successful negotiation would be dangerous enough because it would inevitably involve concessions. Rights and interests of the Palestinians would have to be traded in any realistic deal. The outcome would be far from perfect from the Arab standpoint. And if the King bore the responsibility for the negotiation he would be bitterly criticized for every imperfection by Palestinians, by his Arab rivals, and by those, like the Saudis, who would blow with the winds of Arab indignation.

An unsuccessful negotiation would weaken him as well. Not only would he have transgressed against Arab solidarity and gone against the hard-liners who say that only force will work, but he would have failed. His prestige and credibility would suffer. And more than his personal credibility is at stake. As a prominent East Banker parliamentarian expresses it: "We Jordanians have our capital—our prestige, our good name, and so forth—and we do not want to squander it in a futile effort to make peace."

At another level, the reality with which the Jordanians were dealing was much more complex and dynamic than such a comparing of risks would suggest. A number of basic issues, not so often articulated, underlie any policy debate about the consequences for Jordan's future of alternative courses of action.

The situation, to begin with, is not simply one in which the Palestinian question awaits resolution. Seen from Amman, the relationship among Jordan, the West Bank, and Israel has settled over the years into a kind of *modus vivendi*, a way of living with a reality that is in principle unacceptable but that in practical terms has seemed without better alternatives. This is not to say that the situation has been static—the West Bank has been steadily slipping into the Israeli pocket throughout the period. But, however regrettable this might be from the standpoint of Jordanians and West Bankers, it has not fundamentally affected the the manner in which the three-way relationship is managed.

Goods and people move from the West Bank into and out of Israel and Jordan. There has been no significant violence along the boundaries of these three entities for sixteen years, not even during the 1973 Arab-Israeli war, when the Jordan valley between the Israeli-occupied West Bank and Jordan seemed almost bizarrely oblivious to the bitter war being fought to the north and south. King Hussein has continued to meet with Israeli leaders with some regularity, as Abdallah did before him. These secret talks have produced no moves toward peace, nor even the resolution of serious immediate problems of the day. They have served, nevertheless, to keep communications open at the top between the two governments responsible for managing the situation on the ground.

Moreover, it is by no means clear that any realistically conceivable solution to the Palestinian question would solve Jordan's domestic Palestinian problem. Whatever threat is posed by the Palestinians for Jordanian stability and continued Hashemite rule lies fundamentally in the demography of the situation. The monarchy and somewhat more than a million East Bankers are inescapably involved, directly, with almost two and a half million Palestinians in Jordan, the West Bank and Gaza and indirectly with over a million more elsewhere in the Middle East. Under most future courses of events, as the Palestinian question continues to churn and evolve, these figures and the sheer ineluctability of Jordan's involvement will tell over the long run.

The solution proposed by the King in 1972—a confederation of Jordan and a West Bank-Gaza Palestinian entity—could pose its own dangers for the monarchy. The Palestinians in Jordan have to varying degrees, depending on their individual circumstances and experiences, become part of Jordanian society. In a federation with Palestinians across the river, who have not shared this process, they might find themselves to be more Jordanian than Palestinian. On the other hand, they might not. In the latter case there might be the temptation at some point for all the Palestinians in both parts of the federation to challenge the rule of the Hashemites. Which way would the Palestinian population of the East Bank be drawn in such a federal arrangement, toward further cohesion with the East Bankers or a reassertion of their common origins with the Palestinians across the river?

Some would argue that the *modus vivendi* since 1970 not only is the safest situation for Jordan but is in fact all the solution that can be expected in this imperfect world, at least until some basic changes alter the political equations in the region. There is something to be said for this point of view. Conventional notions of a peace settlement, involving the creation of a Palestinian entity of some sort in territories now occupied by Israel, may have been overtaken by the evolution of the factual situation. Strong groups in Israel oppose surrendering any of the West Bank, and few would agree to surrender all of it. To even the moderate Palestinians, giving up all of Mandate Palestine except for Gaza and the West Bank appears to be sacrifice enough without having the territory whittled down still further. The proliferation of Israeli settlements on the West Bank has severely complicated the problem of reconciling these disparate views. And beyond the territorial issue is the question of the Palestinians who once lived in what is now Israel, and their claims for what they left behind and lost. Many Jordanian citizens are among them.

Jerusalem, too, has if anything become more difficult to resolve. It has always been the most complex and the most passionately regarded issue in the Arab-Israeli conflict. U.S. and Jordanian experts have tended to see it as something that could be solved only after other pieces of the Jordanian-Palestinian-Israeli puzzle fell into place. At that point the pressure on the parties to find an answer to Jerusalem, it has been hoped, would produce the sort of imaginative arrangement that will be necessary if anything is to work. Much of Israel's settlement construction has been in and around Jerusalem, however, and is designed to make such an arrangement as difficult as possible.

The Arab-Israeli conflict has been a continuing lesson in the impossibility of returning to what might have been practicable at an earlier stage. Visions of feasible solutions seem never to keep up with the state of the conflict. The likelihood of failure in any given attempt to make peace raises, therefore, another question mark about the wisdom of trying.

In terms of Jordan's domestic integrity, the current *modus vivendi*, if it can be maintained, might seem to avoid the riskier courses of events. Continued ambiguity and lack of resolution may not be as dangerous as most alternative futures.

What is worrying, though, is whether it can be maintained. Changes which have been taking place may threaten the *modus vivendi* itself. It may not, therefore, be a comfortable alternative to a risky enterprise. The absence of a settlement, or hope for one, has had corrosive effects. The advocacy of more extreme Israeli solutions and the outbreak of Palestinian violence against Israelis on the West Bank in 1984 and 1985 are examples close to home. More widely, thoughout the region, there has been a tendency toward violent solutions to problems. The Syrian government's solution to an uprising in the Syrian city of Hama in February 1982, for example, was so brutal that it added to the Middle East lexicon a new term for unlimited violence: playing by Hama rules.

It may be that attempts to negotiate peace, however likely or unlikely they may be to succeed, are necessary to shore up the *modus vivendi*, are in fact a part of it. Maintaining some focus on the possibility of peace may encourage conduct conducive to peace and help forstall the resort to violent ways of breaking out of an unacceptable reality.

A parallel can be found on the wider canvas of the entire region. The Middle East is in a continuing process of change and evolution. Some Jordanians speak of the unresolved shape and character of the Arab World, where past forms have failed and new ones are being sought. They believe that an insistence on peaceful means, on moderation as a mode of political life, even by a few voices, can affect the shaping process that is going on.

Jordanian Strategy

Faced with many imponderables and many risks, Hussein has adopted over the years a cautious strategy. He has taken a positive stance toward peace with Israel and a compromise settlement of the Palestinian problem. He has never been a rejectionist, refusing to reach an accommodation with Israel. In practice, however, he has in the past wanted some advance guarantee of a negotiating outcome that would be at least minimally favorable from his point of view. Without that, he has considered it too risky to venture very far into a negotiating process.

In 1984 the King and his advisers decided that the arguments for taking a new diplomatic peace initiative outweighed those against it so long as certain safeguards could be built in. It is difficult to say what considerations weighed most heavily with the King: the appeals of the West Bankers; the concern that the West Bank was fast disappearing as a negotiable issue; his feeling of responsibility for the Palestinians under Israeli occupation and for Jerusalem; a desire to keep the focus on the West Bank and Gaza as the Palestinian homeland rather than on Jordan; concern that domestic tensions might grow in the absence of a settlement; a yearning for center stage; the need to refurbish his credentials in Washington as an advocate of peace with Israel, in part to position himself for an arms purchase from the United States; a sense that the *modus vivendi* since 1967 was unraveling; a belief that, refined calculations aside, the worst perils lay in a future without peace. All probably contributed.

The initiative that emerged was bolder than past strategies in that it no longer insisted on advance assurances of a favorable outcome. The King was persuaded that the situation called for more of a commitment on his part if he was to have a chance of being taken seriously in Washington. He knew American support was essential for success.

In other respects the new strategy represented a compromise between conservatives among the King's advisers and those who advocated the taking of greater risks. The Jordanians believed it would reduce to an acceptable level the threat from Syria and other forces likely to oppose the initiative, and would leave the King relatively unweakened should the effort fail.

The three men who worked most closely with the King in devising the strategy were all in their mid-fifties, about Hussein's age; all were experienced in government and diplomacy. All were very much Western-oriented.

Adnan Abu Odeh, a Palestinian, had long been a one-man think-tank for the King and was now Minister of the Royal Court. Articulate, persuasive, an innovator and conceptualizer on a broad scale, he thinks in a way familiar to Western intellectuals. He spent 1975–76 as an International Fellow at Harvard, and his strategic thinking owes something to that experience. He argues for the need to change attitudes on the Israeli side by Arab actions that show a clear commitment to peaceful, negotiated solutions. He is a strong believer in the dynamics of negotiations, of the changes that could be brought about in both the PLO and Israel by a serious negotiating process. These are ideas not often encountered among Arabs or, indeed, among Israelis, both of whom tend to take the other side as a fixed, unchangeable and hostile monolith.

An adviser of a more conservative stamp, influential in the hammering out of Jordan's strategy, is Marwan Qasem, Chief of the Royal Court, an East Banker by family background and personal conviction. His father had been in the Ottoman army and joined Abdallah in the 1920s (*his* father had been a Palestinian), and his mother was a Circassian. He has a personal interest in the early reign of King Abdallah and spends some of his little free time gathering documents from the period. Qasem is a strong advocate of the view that the Palestinians and not Jordan should bear the responsibility for decisions affecting the West Bank and Gaza in any peace negotiation.

A third influential figure is Rifai, whose family background was described in Chapter 2. Educated at Columbia and Harvard Universities, he is a political pragmatist. At the time when Jordan's strategy was being worked out he had no governmental office except for the vice presidency of the upper house of Parliament. He managed his large, modern farm in the Jordan valley and acted as informal adviser to the King. He is a close personal friend of Hussein from boyhood days, and when he became Prime Minister in early 1985, his became an influential voice in shaping and carrying out the peace initiative. His influence would tend to frame a cautious policy, especially wary of pushing Syria into too great a sense of isolation, with the dangers that would pose for Jordan. He is known for his belief in the importance of Jordan's ties with Syria.

Others in the King's circle with influence in the design of the initiative and actions flowing from it included, notably, General Zeid ben Shaker, Commander of the Jordanian Army. He and his family, Hashemites themselves, go back a long way with the family of the King. The General's grandfather, Sharif Zeid ben Fawaz, was a close friend and counselor of Hussein ibn Ali, King of the Hejaz. Ben Shaker's father, Sharif Shaker ben Zeid, fought alongside Abdallah in the Hejaz during World War I. General Zeid ben Shaker himself has been close to King Hussein throughout his career. As a captain and aide he accompanied Hussein on his crucial ride to Zarqa to quell the army mutiny in April 1957. He represents a conservative point of view in the King's councils, especially wary of dealing with the PLO.

The major feature of the King's initiative was his insistence that the PLO do the negotiating for the Palestinians. It was often remarked in the Palace at the time the strategy was being hammered out that only the Palestinians themselves could make concessions on the West Bank or Gaza, such as trading away territory or agreeing to some Israeli settlements remaining in areas turned back to Arab control. The King could not. This provision, of course, made it easier for Hussein to drop his requirement for advance guarantees of a favorable outcome; here the Palestinians would bear the responsibility for the most risky part of the negotiations.

As the King envisioned it, the negotiations would be embedded in and evolve out of an international conference that included the Soviet Union and Syria. In part the conference would provide political cover for Jordan. In part also Hussein believed Moscow and Damascus could be serious threats as spoilers if they were not included. He remembered Andropov's hostility to his 1982–83 effort. By the same token, he felt that a Soviet Union that was taken into the game would help bring the PLO and Syria along.

The opening gun in Jordan's initiative had to be aimed at the PLO. Without Arafat the peace effort would go nowhere. While the King failed in 1982–83, this time Arafat was less likely to refuse. As one Jordanian observer put it, Arafat would just be a man in the street in Tunis if the Jordanians had not given him this opportunity.

King Hussein's peace initiative and Arafat's search for ways to re-establish his pre-eminence came together in the meeting of the PLO's Palestinian National Council in late 1984. Arafat badly needed to hold the meeting to reassert his authority, but he had difficulty finding a site. He was out of favor in some of the usual places. It suited Jordan's purpose to have it in Amman. It was an opportunity to kick off the King's attempt to win PLO support and to assert the maximum Jordanian influence over the PLO.

Some East Bankers opposed playing host to Arafat's conference; General Zeid ben Shaker was one of those who recalled 1970 and worried about giving the PLO another chance to get a foothold in Amman. An associate of the King conceded at the time that the PLO would have liked to come back in force, but said that the King was fully alive to the danger. He wanted to keep Arafat as a guest in Amman, no more than that. "Let him use the royal guest house all he wants," commented this observer. While some PLO infrastructure moved in, the King believed he had struck a balance in which he achieved some control over the PLO without allowing the organization to assemble nearly the strength it would need to be a problem again.

The PNC meeting, held in November 1984, was a success from Jordan's point of view. In his opening speech King Hussein threw down a challenge to the PLO to put aside its hesitancy and discord and get on with the urgent business of solving the Palestinian problem. "There is either the will and the determination to act or there is not," he said. History would record the PLO's answer, he concluded, because in it lay the "last feasible chance to save the land, the people and the holy places." And to solve the Palestinian problem, the King made clear, it was necessary for the PLO as well as Jordan to adhere to U.N. Resolution 242, something the PLO had always been unwilling to do.

In the weeks following the meeting the Jordanians pressed Arafat to agree to a specific formulation describing a common Jordanian-PLO understanding of the peace initiative. They wanted to bind Arafat to the beginnings of a position that might be acceptable to the United States and give Israeli moderates something to work with in building support for compromise on the West Bank. Finally, on February 11, 1985, Arafat agreed to a carefully worded set of points that the Jordanians believed gave them a credible first step. Among the points was acceptance of the exchange of land for peace, the basic deal of U.N. Resolution 242.

Jordanian leaders did not deceive themselves that Arafat had become a loyal convert to their peace initiative. They realized that his acquiescence was a tactical move to get himself out of the box he was in. In their eyes he was a leader whose first priority was to stay in power and in prominence, not to settle the Palestinian problem. The more cynical among them believed, in fact, that he and his lieutenants ("all those Abu's" as one Jordanian called them, referring to their affectation of taking second names in the Arab form that actually means "father of"; Arafat is Abu Amar) realized they might have neither jobs nor glory if the problem were settled.

As the year wore on, Arafat's conduct did nothing to reassure the Jordanians. The hijacking of an Italian cruise ship in October seemed to show Arafat still engaging in terrorism and severely damaged his credibility in Europe and the United States as well as with the Jordanian leadership. At about the same time, he backed out of a carefully prepared arrangement for two PLO representatives to sign a declaration renouncing terrorism and accepting Israel's right to exist. The declaration was a precondition for a meeting of the two PLO men with the British Foreign Secretary, worked out in advance by Hussein, who saw it as a major step in legitimizing the PLO for a peace conference role.

The Syrian threat had been a preoccupation in Amman throughout the planning for a diplomatic initiative on the Palestinian question. The Jordanians had thought to reduce it to manageable proportions by the partnership with Arafat, widely regarded as the legitimate Palestinian leader; by obtaining the endorsement of a broad spectrum of the Arab world, especially Saudi Arabia; and by building into the initiative an international conference that would include Syria and the Soviet Union. Two of these three safeguards were falling short by the end of the year. Arafat, as we have seen, proved an unconvincing partner. The Saudis and other Arabs were anything but enthusiastic about the King's efforts. An Arab League Council Summit that was convened in Morocco in August to consider it failed to agree on endorsement, contenting itself with a platitudinous "blessing" for Jordanian-PLO cooperation. The Saudi king did not even attend, sending Crown Prince Abdullah to represent Saudi Arabia. The third safeguard, the concept of an international conference, fared better. It met a hesitant reception in Washington, and Israel's reaction was at best cool, but both the American and Israeli governments sought ways to give a broader international dimension to a peace negotiation.

With his insurance policies against Syrian interference in such disarray, Hussein moved directly to repair his relationship with Damascus. In a dramatic gesture he acknowledged that the Muslim Brotherhood agitation against the Syrian regime in the early 1980s had been supported from within Jordan. An open letter from the King to Prime Minister Rifai appeared in the Jordanian press November 10, 1985, condemning subversion against Syria that was "disguised in the cloak of our sacred religion." It was generally regarded in Jordan as directed primarily against Muslim fundamentalists, in particular the Muslim Brotherhood.[1]

At the same time, through Saudi intercession, Rifai met directly with the Syrian leadership. Based on his groundwork, Hussein himself was in Damascus by year's end for a meeting with Assad. The Syrian-Jordanian relationship appeared to be headed back toward the warmth

---

[1]In addition to proffering an olive branch to Damascus, the King's move gave him a convenient excuse to rein in some of the more extreme Muslim fundamentalists who posed problems domestically, including Muslim Brotherhood extremists who had been drifting across the line into forbidden political waters.

that had characterized it in the mid- and late 1970s. It remained to be seen how far the process would go, how long it would last, and what effect it would have on the prospects for peace negotiations.

Whatever the longer-term prospects for Hussein's peace initiative, it seemed in ensuing months to be enabling Jordan to gain some influence over events. It helped set an agenda on which peace and moderation were given high priority. The United States was taking the Jordanian effort seriously and Washington was engaging itself. Israeli Prime Minister Peres was pressing ahead on a parallel track. The opening to Damascus no doubt owed something to the momentum of the peace diplomacy.

Hussein faced a dilemma with respect to the Palestinians, however. While Arafat's behavior made him and the PLO less and less acceptable as negotiating partners, the Palestinians on the West Bank and in Gaza continued to insist that the PLO was for them a necessary player in reaching a settlement. While many of them no doubt privately deplored the PLO's inability to be serious about negotiating peace, they had no alternative representation to turn to. A prominent West Banker was quoted in the October 27 *Washington Post*, after the hijacking of the Italian ship, as saying, "There is a concerted campaign by Peres, and backed by the United States, to stereotype Arafat and the PLO as terrorists. They think they can sow dissension between the Palestinians and Jordan and get separate Israeli-Jordanian peace talks. This is wishful thinking." The *Post* correspondent commented that "With stunning unanimity the unofficial spokesmen for the Arab community [on the West Bank] flatly rejected the notion of peace talks without the PLO and Arafat."

The familiar question was again on the agenda in Amman: whether to let the PLO scuttle the peace diplomacy or to find some way to proceed without it, or at least without Arafat. Would an alternative PLO leadership backed by Syria, say, be acceptable to Palestinian communities in the West Bank, Gaza, and elsewhere in the Arab world? Was it conceivable that another leadership, especially one in the good graces of Damascus, would make the conciliatory moves necessary to give any chance of a place at the negotiating table? Syria had not been distinguished for backing moderate PLO factions.

Hussein's choice, in the end, was to break off efforts with the PLO, accusing Arafat of bad faith. In a February 19, 1986, speech he said Jordan "once again" turned "the matter over to the Palestinian fora in the occupied territories and the diaspora as well as Arab capitals and organizations." If he had expected West Bankers to come forward to represent

Palestinians in place of the PLO he was likely to be disappointed. The assassination of the moderate West Bank Arab mayor of Nablus eleven days later, apparently by Palestinian extremists, would have confirmed West Bankers in their customary refusal to play such a role.

Even if the Jordanian-Palestinian effort could be revived there lay ahead the very open question whether any genuine solution of the larger Palestinian issue is practicable. The Jordanians understand this, some more than others to be sure. As they launched their initiative they saw a long process ahead. One of the Palace advisers spoke of a "negotiation that proceeds with stops and starts for a long time." Interim agreements might be arrived at along the way. Accompanying the negotiation, in his view, would have to be an educational process that tried to change the climate of opinion and emotion in which the problem was thought about on the two sides.

Ultimately, however, such a result cannot be achieved with mirrors, as another leading Jordanian points out. Without some idea of a solution, however distant, that appears credible to the people on both sides and some concrete steps toward it, the momentum will flag. It is true that what seems impossible today may become possible tomorrow if attitudes can be changed. And they can be changed to some degree by believable professions of peaceful intent by the respective leaders. But sooner or later the process will require some vision of an outcome that could satisfy the main groups involved, and there is the rub. For, as we have seen, if the focus remains essentially two-dimensional— the allotment of disputed territory to Israel and to the Arabs—an agreed outcome is extremely difficult to envision.

Only when other ingredients are put into the mix does there appear to be the prospect of an eventual solution of sorts. The idea of phasing, of interim stages to permit confidence to grow on both sides, is one that has been much thought about. It is in fact embodied in the Camp David agreement about negotiating a future for the West Bank and Gaza. More fundamentally, the West Bank and Gaza may well have to have a relationship to both Jordan and Israel that is unique and departs from standard concepts of the "this is mine, that is yours" distribution of territory.

Some West Bank businessmen and professionals, accustomed to dealing with Israelis, advocate continuing ties with the Jewish state in any settlement and feel self-confident about holding their own against Israelis in such an arrangement. The idea of a joint Israeli-Jordanian condominium for the West Bank and Gaza has been talked about in the past, but it sounds too much like replacing a single occupation with a double one to appeal much to Palestinians. If the concept could be expanded to include a more active Palestinian role, it might be more palatable. The West Bank particularly does seem destined by history and geography to be a mediator and go-between for the Jewish and Arab societies that flank it.

As for Jerusalem, a straightforward division into Arab and Israeli sections seems even less promising a possibility. A unique and imaginative regime will be required if the competing nationalist and religious claims to the holy city are to be reconciled—perhaps a regime that tries to finesse a clash of national sovereignties by emphasizing local administration of the city.

Even given the most imaginative approach to a settlement, the prospect is not encouraging. The future of the entire region—the Arab-Israeli cockpit, Lebanon, the Persian Gulf—is unpredictable and laced with possibilities for change and violence. Renewed conflict between Syria and Israel, for example, would wipe peace talks off the agenda for some time at least. More basically, the Middle East is still evolving lasting configurations. The shocks and pressures of the past seventy years have been immense. This is the long-run reality the Jordanian leaders must deal with. They must focus first on husbanding the strength and cohesiveness the country has developed, but they must reach out at the same time to help shape the political environment that is developing around them. The United States, too, in its policies toward the region must give careful attention to both dimensions.

7

Conclusions—And
Thoughts about U.S. Policy

The answer to the American journalist whose question introduced these chapters on Jordan is: No, the Palestinians would not simply take over if Hussein and Hassan disappeared; Jordan is not a Palestinian state waiting to happen. But Yes, Jordan is likely over time to reflect a growing influence of the Palestinian majority—a majority that will probably increase.

The kingdom's history is entwined with that of the Palestinian people, but it has a separate existence and identity of its own. If the Palestinian problem, as King Hussein has said, is Jordan's main preoccupation, the country is nevertheless not defined by it.

Jordan has developed a characteristic economic system and distinctive domestic social and political relationships, different from those of other Middle East countries. They represent a mix of considerable personal freedom and the generally sensible hand of a paternalistic state. By regional standards all are marked by relatively low levels of tension. The two most important institutions in the country—the monarchy and the army—also bear a distinctive Jordanian stamp.

While the division of the population into a large East Banker minority and a slight Palestinian majority is a source of potential instability, both groups today are incorporated in a composite society that can only be called Jordanian. The Palestinians retain a sense of separate identity, but the more affluent and especially the young have ties to the common society that increasingly transcend their particularity. For the Palestinians these ties may be of the mind rather than the heart, but they are there.

It is true that so long as the larger, regional Palestinian question remains open, Jordanian society will also in a sense be unresolved. This uncertainty notwithstanding, Jordan is a state and is becoming a nation. It has experienced tremendous stresses and has proved durable. It is firmly enough established so that it would persist as an entity through changes in government or economic system, although the moderate, Western-oriented character and the stability that have marked it might well be altered in the process.

The Hashemite monarchy is less durable than the state, but there is no reason to foresee its disappearance. The institution of the monarchy and the person of the King are supported by powerful forces in the country, especially the army. No important body of opinion wants the overthrow of the monarchy and its replacement with another form of government. The succession would be a delicate time for the monarchy, but for the near future, barring a radical change in circumstances, the army can be expected to ensure the transition to another Hashemite ruler.

To be sure, modernization has created social and political tensions. An increasingly prosperous and educated middle class, heavily but not solely Palestinian, questions the King's paternalistic style of rule. There is some pressure for more representative government, both out of a desire to participate and because firmer institutions of government would make the system more durable.

The pressure does not seem likely to be destabilizing, however. Nor does it appear likely that this King will be prepared to surrender enough power to give life to representative institutions. Some thoughtful Jordanians, in fact, question whether the standard democratic forms of government would work for Jordan.

Attempts from inside or outside the country to replace the monarchy with a Palestinian government would be met with fierce resistance from the army, the intelligence service (the GID) and the East Banker establishment. But there seems little or no disposition on the part of the Palestinian majority in the country to take over the government. The social contract by which the King provides the secure and stable context in which the citizenry can live securely and make money has appeal for the middle class especially.

Over the longer run, however, it seems inevitable that Jordan will in some way come to reflect the weight of Palestinian numbers in the region, whatever route such a process takes. In the absence of a peace settlement, Jordan will likely absorb more Palestinians, who will gradually acquire more political influence over time. If Jordan, on the other hand, is linked by a peace settlement to the West Bank and Gaza, the population arithmetic of the combined entity would almost certainly also result at a minimum in greater influence by Palestinians, perhaps in a shorter period of time.

What is crucial for the peace and stability of the country and region is that these processes take place gradually rather than suddenly and traumatically. Much can be changed by evolution, and Jordan does have the plasticity to absorb some change. A Hashemite successor to Hussein could conceivably reign as a more limited monarch over a Jordan dominated by people of Palestinian origin but integrated into a plural Jordanian society. Over time Palestinian and East Banker identities may lose much of their meaning in domestic affairs of the country, especially if the regional Palestinian question is resolved peacefully and if economic or political distress does not suddenly bring a large influx of Palestinians from the Gulf back to Jordan.

Despite the uncertainties about various solutions and their effects on Jordan, it is important that efforts to resolve the Palestinian problem continue whether or not they succeed. A solution, with all its unknowns, would be a better bet for Jordan and the region than continuation of the past *modus vivendi*. While some forms of a peace settlement could bring new dangers of their own, the worst potential dangers lie down the road of no settlement and no peace. And even if the peace efforts continue to fail, they may well be necessary to keep the *modus vivendi* from unraveling. This may be one status quo that, to endure, must include continuing efforts to change it. If hope for a negotiated solution dries up, more extreme ways of relieving the pressures the problem brings for Israel, Jordan and the Palestinians are more likely to be tried.

For all its proven durability, Jordan remains vulnerable to external interference and dependent on external support. Its most evident dependence is economic; gaps in its balance of payments and budget cannot be closed without outside subsidies in some form. It is also politically vulnerable to stronger neighbors and ultimately must rely on outside help—political or military—to protect it from military attack.

By virtue of its strategic location as a buffer, and because its moderate, pro-Western character has commended it to important Western powers, it has been able to balance these weaknesses. In addition, it has shown itself adroit in exploiting the rivalries of its stronger neighbors with one another.

U.S. Policy and Commitment

One of A. A. Milne's books about Winnie the Pooh opens with the child Christopher Robin coming downstairs dragging Pooh behind him by the heel. As Pooh's head bounces from step to step, he thinks to himself, in effect, "I'm sure there is a better way of coming downstairs if only my head would stop bumping long enough for me to think about it." Milne's lines bring to mind American policy in the Middle East. Hammered by recurring crises of sudden violence, constrained by strong domestic political pressures, Washington has seldom had the luxury of the long view.

To the extent that a broad strategic framework for policy has relevance in the Middle East, it could well start from the point at which the previous chapter ended: This is a region in ferment, working its way toward forms of social and political organization not yet clear.

Despite the appearance of greater stability today, after the major changes in the years from 1945 to the early 1970s, the region does not give the impression of having come to rest. The Arabs have not come to terms with their weakness and inability to cope with Israel and the West. The Palestinian problem is a continuing reminder of this and contains pressures of its own as well. Radical Islamic currents, set in motion partly by this same sense of failure and frustration, may well not have run their course. The poor and the powerless in Arab societies may see in the sudden ascendancy of the Shiites in Lebanon an example for themselves. The future impact of a more aggressive and assertive Israel, if right-wing forces come into control again, is unpredictable. The region's economies are vulnerable to sudden change in the price of a few products, particularly oil.

Change spurred by these forces could produce a Middle East considerably more difficult for the United States to relate to than the region of today. A new wave of social, economic and political unrest could lead to increased hostility to the West and the United States in particular, as has happened in Iran, but it could also provide an opening for the Soviet Union to enhance its power position at U.S. expense.

Tempting though the idea tends to seem to Americans, there is no way to freeze the status quo. Change will occur. Moreover, outside countries—even the United States—have at best a limited capacity to influence this process since the future of the Middle East will be shaped largely by the people of the region. Within these limitations, American policy should do what it can to encourage stable, gradual change. It should help reduce sources of tension and future violence that endanger our friends and push the region in radical, anti-Western directions.

Jordan is important in the pursuit of this goal. Though it is small and dependent, the success of its policy, the prosperity of its social, economic and political system, and indeed its mere survival in its present form all weigh in the regional balance on the positive side in the evolution of a Middle East in which peace, moderation and the effective use of economic resources provide a better life for its people. This is especially, or at least more predictably, so under Hashemite leadership. It would be less so, for example, if that leadership were replaced by an unstable parliamentary government or a military regime without legitimacy. The United States thus has an interest in the survival of the monarchy as well.

Beyond its long-term importance as an example and a force for moderation, Jordan has more immediate consequence in its roles as a stabilizing buffer among hostile states, as a security factor in the Gulf region, and as an indispensable participant in the management of the Palestinian problem.

If it is to play these roles successfully, Jordan needs strong and continuing support from the United States. The relationship is very much a two-way street. A basic, long-term commitment is required, a commitment to Jordan as a state important to the United States, not a commitment that is dependent on the current status of the Palestinian problem or the U.S. relationship with Israel.

The U.S. government has in fact recognized an informal commitment to Jordan since the late 1950s. There have been times, however, when it has seemed to the Jordanians to wear quite thin. U.S. responses to Jordanian requests for weapons are the most obvious example. Another was the period after Camp David. President Jimmy Carter's pique at Hussein's predictable refusal to take part in the process that had been worked out by others led him to put U.S. relations with the King in deep freeze. Part of the value of a commitment is that the state concerned, and other states as well, remain in no doubt about it.

In practical terms, U.S. support for and collaboration with Jordan touch three areas primarily: political—involving principally the Palestinian problem and peace with Israel; security—that of Jordan itself and the Gulf; and economic—Jordan's economic viability.

Politics of Arab-Israeli Conflict

The dominating concern of U.S.-Jordanian relations over the years has been the Arab-Israeli dispute in all of its layers and dimensions. It is the arena in which Washington and Amman have the most to offer, and require of, each other. For both it has meant not only regional peace or war, but also Jordan's well-being as a nation and state. For the United States, in addition, it has involved the security of Israel and the competition with the Soviet Union.

The relationship has had a firm foundation of shared goals for the most part. Both the United States and Jordan have wanted a settlement of the conflict, and since 1967 both have envisioned a settlement in somewhat similar terms. In Washington as in Amman, the focus has been on the deal made in U.N. Resolution 242, the return of the occupied territories for peace. Both capitals have seen a major role for Jordan in a settlement for the West Bank and more recently for Gaza as well. Neither has wanted a Palestinian state.

In these respects the United States and Jordan have been closer to the views of the Israeli Labor Party than to those of the Palestinian national movement and most Arab governments, which have pressed for a separate Palestinian state. As to the amount of territory to be returned to Arab control, the United States has stood somewhere between the Labor Party and Jordan, though closer to the Jordanian view.

The collaboration between Washington and Amman has been strained, however, by misconceptions and misplaced expectations. For years Hussein expected the United States to deliver Israel's agreement to withdraw from the West Bank in accordance with Resolution 242 without his having to stick his neck out in open-ended negotiations. The United States, for its part, has envisioned a classical negotiating process in which Jordan would go up against Israel and get the best deal it could. Washington argued that only in the context of such a process could it give Hussein the backing he felt he needed for an outcome close to what he and the United States thought just. Washington also persisted in expecting Jordan to negotiate for the Palestinians even after 1974, when this became far too risky for the King.

The air was considerably clearer on these issues as Hussein launched his 1985 initiative. He had lost his illusions about the U.S. willingness or ability to deliver Israel, and Washington largely accepted that the King had to keep Palestinians out ahead of him on Palestinian issues.

The United States accommodated itself only gingerly, however, to Hussein's insistence on an international conference (to include both the Soviet Union and Syria) as a larger context for peace negotiations.

The proposal touched sensitive nerves in Washington. Including the Soviet Union in a conference on the Middle East has tended to be seen by the more conservative American policy-makers as "bringing the Soviets into the region." The deeply conservative Reagan Administration especially has found this an unsetttling thought. Washington has also been disturbed by the prospect of Syria's participation. Strong Israeli reservations on both counts, while not the basis for U.S. concerns, have reinforced them.

To be sure, the Soviet Union and Syria would be a complicating presence at a peace conference. Their uncompromising support for a hard-line Arab position would make bargaining difficult. They seem to pose a truly major problem, however, only if one would expect and prefer a negotiation that produced a partial settlement, on the order of Camp David—presumably in this case an arrangement for the West Bank and Gaza alone. This kind of settlement would be ruled out by their presence. Syria could not be expected to participate in the solution of the West Bank and Gaza issue, for example, without insisting that the matter of its own territory—the Golan Heights—be on the agenda as well. Both Syria and the Soviet Union, moreover, would want a settlement of all aspects of the Palestinian problem, including the claims of Palestinians for properties lost in pre-1967 Israel.

But such a settlement—Camp David II as it is called by the Arabs—is not in the cards in any case. Hussein knows he could not pull it off without grave risk to his political survival. Indeed, designing an international conference into his initative was a way of reassuring the rest of the Arab World that he had no intention of trying to do so.

Washington, after an initially negative reaction, seemed to recognize that the Soviet Union and Syria cannot be excluded, and has considered various ways to include them without turning the negotiation into a Versailles-style peace conference. This is realistic. Limiting a negotiation to the West Bank and Gaza is not feasible. Conceivably a comprehensive settlement of the Palestinian problem would be acceptable in the Arab world without in the same stage settling the Golan issue between Syria and Israel, so long as Syria had a hand in it. This could only become evident in the working out of the negotiation. But the United States would be wise to encourage as broad a negotiation as the Arabs seem to require, since otherwise there will be no settlement of any part of the problem.

Washington should show the same understanding of moves by Hussein to repair relations with Syria. Past such efforts, as in the mid-1970s, have caused concern especially among supporters of Israel who feared that Jordan would be drawn into Syria's hard-line position. This has not happened, nor is it likely to. Hussein, if anything, is seeking greater latitude and security for his own policies. The American tendency to equate Syria and the Soviet Union, and to see Syria therefore as an ideological opponent in the Middle East, has been a blind spot in U.S. policy. Syria is, to be sure, an uncomfortable presence in the area—all the more so because of the patient competence with which Syrian President Hafez el-Assad plays his hand. As the major Arab power in that part of the Middle East, however, Syria must be reckoned with. It would be a mistake for Washington to consign it to the enemy camp. Hussein's approach to Damascus is an opportunity for the United States to draw Syria more actively into its own diplomacy in the region.

If the United States is to have influence over the future of the region, it is important for Washington to remain firmly involved in the Arab-Israeli problem, working closely with Jordan and Israel. There have always been those who argued that the United States should stay on the sidelines; the Israelis themselves have pressed such a view at times. But whether or not negotiations are held, and whether or not they succeed if they are held, the set of issues embraced in the Arab-Israeli conflict largely defines the most important relationships in this part of the Middle East. Working together with Jordan and Israel, the United States can help the parties most directly involved to steer these relationships into constructive or at least minimally destructive channels.

This being said, the United States nevertheless also has to avoid the illusion that its influence extends to the point of control. The Middle East states themselves make the running. Without the help of the United States they might not succeed—witness Camp David—but without political commitment on their part there is no horserace at all.

If negotiations are at some point gotten underway, the process is likely to be long, difficult and intermittent. Other developments in the area will threaten to derail them, in some cases intentionally, as opponents of accommodation stir up trouble. The United States can be a steadying influence, strengthening the hand of the King and of the moderates in Israel.

The need for the United States to stay close and active will not fade if a settlement is eventually reached. Profound changes will very likely result, with unpredictable consequences. Substantial forces in the region may be opposed to the settlement, whatever it is. Hussein may go through a delicate period until the new forms jell. Even then, some settlement arrangements could expose him and the stability of Jordan to new pressures. The United States will certainly undertake a strong commitment to the success of any peace settlement, and Jordan will be a crucial factor in carrying out such a commitment. The American stake in Jordan may grow rather than diminish.

If negotiations fail, there could be a swing back toward violence and despair. Depending on the circumstances, the Jordanians themselves might overreact, as they were tempted to do after the 1974 Rabat summit. The King's position would be weakened and Jordan's moderate course called into question. The United States again would want to remain closely involved to limit the damage. Above all, Americans should avoid recriminations against Jordan for the failure. Ideally, of course, Washington should make every effort, as it has in the past, to avoid a definitive collapse of the peace process by resorting to devices to buy time, allow reassessment of the options, and so forth. The Jordanians, some of the King's advisers especially, would likely be sympathetic to such efforts.

A special problem for the United States in dealing with the Palestinian problem has been its relationship with the Palestinians themselves. In the first instance this has meant its relationship with the PLO.

Largely at Israeli insistence, Washington has refused to negotiate with or recognize the PLO unless the organization accepts U.N. Resolution 242 and acknowledges Israel's right to exist. The United States has formally committed itself to hold to these preconditions.[1] The PLO has been unwilling to agree to either of them.

Friendly Arab governments have in the past urged the United States to open contacts with Arafat as a means of strengthening his hand against the radicals in the PLO. Washington has consistently declined in the absence of PLO agreement to its terms. It has not wished to violate its commitment to Israel nor to unleash the storm of domestic political protest from U.S. supporters of Israel. As international terrorism by Palestinian groups increased in 1985, moreover, broader public opposition would have greeted any effort to establish relations with the PLO.

Even leaving aside the public reaction, a U.S. opening to the PLO

---

[1] It did so in 1975 in an undertaking to Israel that served as an inducement to the Israelis to enter into the second disengagement agreement with Egypt whereby both countries agreed to pull their troops back farther in the Sinai.

would have brought problems. Such a move would enhance Arafat's position and that of the PLO. Their role as representatives of the Palestinians in any negotiation would be fortified. To move matters in this direction, however, when Israel is so highly unlikely at any time to negotiate with the PLO would be to lead the peace process into a blind alley.

The issue of the U.S. attitude toward the PLO became more immediate as Hussein struggled in 1985 to bring a weakened and more isolated Arafat into a diplomatic process leading to the negotiation of a peace settlement with Israel. Arafat had perfected the tactic of escaping from confining situations by finding support elsewhere that enhanced his freedom of action. A direct line to Washington would have given him just such freedom of maneuver, however conditional it might have been on his good behavior, and Israel might well have soured on the Jordanian initiative.

The United States has probably been right to keep the PLO at a distance. To be sure, if negotiations become a genuine prospect, the question of Palestinian participants with legitimacy will be a serious one that the United States will have to face together with Israel and Jordan. There is probably no alternative to the familiar and difficult diplomatic process of identifying Palestinians who are trusted by the PLO and yet can be regarded by Israel as not of the PLO. Regardless of divisions and tensions within its ranks, it does not seem likely that the PLO will fade away in the forseeable future or that it can be ignored.

In a more fundamental sense the United States needs to be concerned about its attitude toward and relationship with the Palestinians as a people and with the national movement, broadly defined. The Palestinians are not inherently radical or hostile to the United States, although there are radical and hostile factions of the PLO. Indeed, it is surprising that so many of them—on the West Bank, in Jordan, and even in the PLO—continue to look to Americans for understanding and friendship when they obviously consider the United States responsible for much of Israel's ability to thwart what they see as justice for their cause.

The U.S. government under the Carter Administration was more understanding of Palestinian aspirations than it had been before. Carter himself spoke of a Palestinian homeland. In the constant tug of war over verbal formulations, Washington had hitherto refused to accept references to "Palestinian rights," insisting on "Palestinian interests" instead. In 1977 it moved for the first time to the use of "legitimate rights" in a joint statement with the Soviet Union; and although that joint statement was quickly consigned to limbo, the same formula appeared later in the Camp David accords. While the Carter Administration did not go so far as to accept Palestinian self-determination, it did acknowledge what it called the need for the Palestinians to participate in the determination of their own future. Reagan's September 1, 1982, Middle East peace proposal indicated that his Administration held essentially to the positions of its predecessor.

It is important to maintain and reiterate a sympathy for the Palestinian people and their rights even while being unable to go all the way in supporting the goal of an independent state. Washington should clearly distinguish between what it objects to in the PLO and its attitude toward the Palestinians generally.

The structure of regional politics does not provide many suitable opportunities for building a better relationship with Palestinians, but the United States should make the most of those that exist. Contacts with the West Bank and Gaza leadership and economic assistance to West Bank and Gaza communities and institutions should be enlarged. At another level, U.S. public positions and declarations should, where possible, be used to help balance the tilt toward Israel that is so predominant, in much more significant ways, in American policy. Washington should stick firmly and publicly to its objections to Israeli settlements in the occupied territories. It should be more prepared to vote with U.N. Security Council majorities against Israeli actions it considers wrong.

American interests are served in a number of ways by relations with the Palestinian community that are at least not hostile. Two advantages especially relate to Jordan. Over the long run, if it seems to be in the cards that Palestinians will become more influential within present-day Jordan or in some form of federated state, this should not be a development that the United States has reason to fear will threaten American interests. Second, from Hussein's point of view, hostility between the United States and the Palestinians could add strains in his own relations with Palestinians under his rule at some future time. He would not benefit from a repetition of the situation that existed before 1956 when the Palestinians sought power in Jordan partly in order to break or reduce the Jordanian connection with a Britain that was considered hostile to Palestinian interests.

When looking toward more extreme and unlikely eventualities— governments must think about the unthinkable—a replacement of the monarchy by a Palestinian-dominated government somewhere well down the road, after Hussein, should not be seen as the end of a constructive U.S.-Jordanian relationship. Continued Hashemite rule assures a more predictable future, from the U.S. point of view, and as such should be strongly supported. It will probably continue indefinitely. But the future of the regime is ultimately not controllable from Washington, and the end of Hashemite rule would not be the end of Jordan nor the end of U.S. relations with Jordan.

Security

A second area of mutual concern and collaboration is security—Jordan's own security and that which it can provide elsewhere in the region.

In protecting itself against external aggression Jordan needs two things of the United States: arms, and assistance in deterring or defeating an attack.

Providing arms poses a difficult problem for the United States. American supporters of Israel, primarily Jewish groups but also, in recent years, right-wing conservatives, see the sale of weapons to Jordan as strengthening a potential enemy of Israel. Through their influence in Congress they can usually prevent a sale or considerably reduce its scale.

Jordan itself has lent support to their arguments by participating in Arab wars against Israel. To argue that domestic and regional pressures make it difficult for the King to stand aside when his Arab brethren are bent on war only strengthens the assumption that he will join in next time as well, if there is a next time.

The United States must obviously consider Israel's security. Americans are paying heavily for it and take it seriously. Given the overwhelming preponderance of Israeli military power, the small-scale, if sophisticated, weapons needs of Jordan appear to be in a different league entirely. But from Israel's perspective every weapon in an Arab hand is bad, particularly if of a high degree of capability that could lesssen Israel's tactical or strategic advantage. But the United States has, or should have, a perspective of its own. Additional weapons systems in some Arab hands may well reinforce U.S. interests without fundamental cost in terms of Israeli security.

This being said, the Israeli perspective is not likely to change nor is American politics. A dilemma is thus posed for the United States. Washington should try to avoid the wrenching contests between the executive branch and the Congress over arms sales that reinforce the impression in Jordan and elsewhere in the Arab World that American policy is controlled by Israel. At the same time, for the United States to reject all requests by Jordan for arms would undermine much of the political-security relationship even though Jordanians can obtain the arms somewhere else. There is no easy answer. Better consultation by the executive with Congress in advance of arms sales proposals might help but would not be a solution. Only when active peace negotiations are underway, or when there is a credible process leading to them, is the Congress likely to view arms sales to Jordan as warranted. Israeli opposition to reasonable Jordanian arms acquisition should diminish, and Congressional concerns about long-term Israeli security would diminish. The considerable support that exists in Congress for Jordan will manifest itself. If Israel still should oppose a sale at such a time, the Administration should press hard with the U.S. public and Congress to free itself from such unacceptable interference.

A full-fledged U.S. commitment to go to Jordan's aid if attack comes is not practicable. But Jordan should be left in no doubt that, short of sending in American forces, the United States will make every effort to assist it to deter or repel an attack that threatens its independence and integrity. While deployment of American forces in Jordan should not be ruled out, especially in a stabilizing role such as the British troops played at the time U.S. Marines went into Lebanon in 1958, it obviously cannot be promised in advance. Nevertheless, intense political efforts can and should be promised.

The Jordanians have reason to assume that they have such a commitment in fact, at least for situations involving threats from Arab states. Washington responded vigorously with diplomatic efforts and warning moves by Sixth Fleet units when Damascus threatened and eventually attacked in 1970. Henry Kissinger, President Richard Nixon's National Security Adviser at the time, describes graphically the intensely serious way in which Jordan's situation and the King's requests for help were regarded. "I had no doubt," writes Kissinger, "that this challenge had to be met."[2] In summing up the crisis, Kissinger writes: "The forces of moderations had been preserved. The King had prevailed by his own courage and decisiveness. Yet these would have been in vain but for his friendship with the United States."[3]

---

[2]Henry Kissinger, *White House Years* (Boston: Little Brown and Co., 1979), p. 618.
[3]*Ibid*, p. 631.

The U.S. ability to help protect Jordan in this way depends, of course, on the capacity of the Jordanian armed forces to hold off or slow an attack. Hence the importance of putting enough weapons in Jordanian hands.

Threats from Israel are a more complex problem, in part because Israel might in some future situation have reason to believe itself threatened by moves on the Jordanian side of the Jordan River. The issue here is perhaps better approached more basically than as simply a matter of Israeli military attack. In the context of the strategic understanding between the United States and Israel, a relationship desired by the Israelis, the United States has a right to insist that Israel not make moves that Washington would see as seriously damaging to U.S. interests in the region. One range of such moves would be those destabilizing to Jordan.

This has no doubt been discussed with Israel. The United States should continue to make clear the importance of its stake in Jordanian stability, especially at times of tension in the area. An outright Israeli attack is only the most extreme possibility. More to the point, especially if Likud hard-liners come back to power, would be such Israeli actions as pressuring large numbers of Arabs to leave the West Bank and Gaza. The Israelis should be left in no doubt that this would be unacceptable to the United States. The United States, in turn, would presumably want to accept, or reaffirm, some responsibility to forestall hostile Jordanian actions against Israel.

It will further reassure Jordan that the United States make clear its support for Jordanian security efforts in the Persian Gulf region. These amount only to training and small-scale secondment of Jordanian army personnel to Gulf states in normal times, but could involve the introduction of large Jordanian forces in some emergencies. A U.S. hand should preferably not be evident in such operations. The Jordanians would have transport problems in moving sizable forces, however, and in urgent operational situations when sufficient transport aircraft were not available from Arab sources, the United States may want to consider with Jordan making some American air transport available.

Economic Support

The third area of U.S. involvement is economic. American economic relations with Jordan are mainly adjuncts of the political and security stake the United States has in the kingdom. The economies of the two countries, as such, have little to do with one another. The United States is not a major trading partner for Jordan—U.S. imports from Jordan are negligible and U.S. products make up only 11 percent of Jordanian imports—and the small Jordanian economy does not provide significant opportunity for investment by Americans. For many years, however, since the British tie with Amman was cut in 1957, Washington has been concerned that Jordan's economic vulnerability would threaten the survival of the country. That concern has been the main basis for American economic policy toward the kingdom.

For more than twenty years after 1957 the United States provided direct support to the Jordanian budget, enabling the King to fill the continuing gap between government income and expenditures and taking some of the pressure off the Jordanian economy generally. British subsidies had played this role earlier. Beginning in 1967, Arab governments supplied major financial support, with some periods of hiatus, and the United States in more recent years has ceased this form of assistance. In 1985, for example, American economic assistance amounted to $20 million for economic projects, $1.876 million for military education and training, and $90 million in credits for the purchase of military equipment in the United States. The Administration's request for 1986 was of the same order of magnitude.

The Administration did, however, attempt to provide budget support funds to Jordan in 1985 as the King's peace initiative was getting underway. During Hussein's June 1985 visit to Washington, President Reagan undertook to give assistance beyond the regular annual appropriation request. A $250 million supplemental request was sent to Congress, containing $100 million for direct budget support. Congress approved the total amount but refused to permit what amounted to a cash grant on the grounds that it might be used to buy arms. Instead, the $250 million was to be provided in the form of project funding and to finance imports of American products by Jordan, the amount to be spread over three years.

So long as Jordan's economic situation remains as it is, with budget and balance-of-payments gaps largely covered by indigenous and regional sources of funding, American aid is useful but not critical. Washington will be faced with serious questions about the level and type of American aid, however, if Jordan's current major sources of income drop so low as to make the country's financial gaps unmanageable. In such a case the American government will have to ask itself whether it can afford to let the crisis run its course and, if it cannot, what actions are available to relieve the pressure.

The first level of response should probably be discussions with the Arab oil states that customarily provide subsidies to Jordan. If the kingdom's problems result from sharp reductions in these subsidies, that might in turn be due either to straitened economic circumstances in the Gulf region or to political pressure by the Gulf governments on Jordan. In either case the United States might suggest that the instability likely to result in Jordan would be a threat to the Gulf monarchies as well as to Jordan itself. If purely economic considerations are involved, Washington could urge a joint effort by the Gulf states to restore a minimum of subsidy sufficient to stave off serious trouble. The United States might offer to participate. If politics lies behind the move, the arguments might be different, but the basic point would be the same. In the latter case, Washington might play a go-between role for Jordan and the Gulf governments.

Precipitate moves by Gulf countries to send home Jordanian workers could arise from the same two causes—economic or political—and could be approached in essentially the same way by the United States.

Any American effort should, of course, be made in consultation with Amman. Such consultation would presumably include as well the consideration of ways for Jordan to cut back on expenses or otherwise mitigate the effects of the shortage. Short-term loans from international lending institutions could be considered, or loans from European governments, the latter being brought into the consultations.

The U.S. contribution to joint efforts could be modest cash grants for budget support, grants to cover food imports from the United States—as were provided in 1985—or credits for the same purpose.

The hardest choice for Washington would come if such diplomatic efforts bore little fruit and an irreducible, major gap remained. The United States would have to consider how much Jordanian stability was at risk and how much it was worth to Americans to avoid that degree of risk. Compared to its very major annual grants to Israel and Egypt, amounts crucial to Jordan would seem limited. Half a billion dollars could be a vital sum in Amman, while amounts several times that much are provided each year to Egypt and Israel. If the purposes of these larger aid programs would in some degree be jeopardized by severe trouble in Jordan, in terms of Israeli security, for example, that would be a factor to consider.

A judgment whether an American subsidy was to tide the Kingdom over a brief rough spot or was likely to be built into the Jordanian economy would be important. If the need was clearly temporary, it is difficult to see how even a subsidy of several hundred million dollars would seem too large, given the U.S. stake in the Middle East. If the need seemed a long-term one, restoration of some U.S. subsidy would probaby still be justified but would have to be accompanied by vigorous efforts to help Jordan attack the underlying problem.

Making foreign policy is or should be a humbling experience. Information about foreign countries is at best fragmentary. Insight into the priorities and motives of foreign leaders is rarely reliable, especially leaders from societies as culturally different from one another as American and Middle Eastern societies. Diplomats tend to see the leaders of foreign countries engaged primarily in a game of chess, or perhaps poker, with one another, whereas the most important game for the average ruler is that which he plays within his own body politic, with his own power as the stake. The rules and imperatives of this internal game are difficult for a foreigner to penetrate, but in the last analysis they largely determine the more visible moves in the game among nations.

For King Hussein the two games interact more critically than for most leaders. Jordan's vulnerability to outside influences, and the fine line between the domestic and the external—almost nonexistent at times—requires the King to use each game carefully for its effects in the other. So much the more difficult becomes the job of the American diplomat.

In Hussein's complex calculation United States policy is important, and in three areas it can be decisive:

- American participation and support is a necessary, though not a sufficient, condition for successful peace negotiations and for the working out of new arrangements that might result.

- American economic support can provide essential underpinning for the state and monarchy when other sources fail.

- The United States can play a critical role in preventing or turning back military aggression against Jordan.

So central are these areas to Jordan's survivability, and so important is Jordan to American policy in the Middle East, that a continuing effort should be made by Americans to understand the domestic dynamics of the country and their influence on its foreign policy. To this purpose these few chapters are dedicated.

Suggested Readings

The historical portions of the book have been based on a variety of published sources, in particular those listed below. The discussion of recent and current conditions and events, as the text itself indicates, is drawn largely from conversation with a wide range of Jordanians and Palestinians, and some Israelis, during two trips to Amman and a visit to the West Bank and Jerusalem during 1985. American scholars, journalists, businessmen and former and current government officials have also provided useful information and insight. *The New York Times*, *The Washington Post*, *The Financial Times* of London and *The Economist* weekly have provided important factual reference points and knowledgeable commentary.

Abdallah ibn Hussein. *Memoirs of King Abdallah of Transjordan*. London: Oxford University Press, 1950.

Abidi, Aqil Hyder. *Jordan: A Political Study, 1948–1967*. New York: Asia Publishing House, 1965.

Aruri, Naseer H. *Jordan: A Study in Political Development (1921–1965)*. The Hague: Martinus Nijhoff, 1972.

Cohen, Amnon. *Political Parties in the West Bank Under the Jordanian Regime, 1949–1967*. Ithaca, N.Y.: Cornell University Press, 1982.

Cordesman, Anthony H. *Jordanian Arms and the Middle East Balance*. Washington, D.C.: Middle East Institute, 1983.

A thorough description and analysis of Jordan's military weaponry and its arms needs, including comparisons with Jordan's principal neighbors in major categories of military strength.

El-Edroos, Brigadier S.A. *The Hashemite Arab Army 1908–1979: An Appreciation and Analysis of Military Operations*. Amman: The Publishing Committee, 1980.

Pakistani Brigadier El-Edroos served as adviser to the Jordan Arab Army in the early 1970s. His study—more than 750 pages long—is replete with maps of military operations and details of the battles participated in by the Hashemites from the Arab Revolt of 1916–18 through the 1973 Arab-Israeli war, and including the conflict with the Palestinian militias in 1970–71.

Glubb, Sir John Bagot. *A Soldier With the Arabs*. New York: Harper, 1957.

Gubser, Peter. *Jordan: Crossroads of Middle Eastern Events*. Boulder, Colo.: Westview, 1983.

Hurewitz, J.C. *The Struggle for Palestine*. New York: Schocken, 1968.

Hussein, King of Jordan. *Uneasy Lies the Head: An Autobiography*. New York: Bernard Geis Associates, 1962.

Ingram, Doreen. *Palestine Papers 1917–1922, Seeds of Conflict*. London: Cox and Wyman Ltd., 1972.

Jureidini, Paul A., and R.D. McLaurin. *Jordan: The Impact of Social Change on the role of the Tribes*. (Published with the Center for Strategic and International Studies, Georgetown University, Washington, D.C.) New York: Praeger, 1984.

Kanovsky, Eliyahu. *The Economic Impact of the Six-day War*. New York: Praeger, 1970.

A much broader and more useful study than the title suggests, the book gives an excellent account of the growth of the East Bank economy, at the expense of that of the West Bank, from 1949 to 1967. It challenges the conventional wisdom that loss of the West Bank was a severe economic blow to Jordan.

Maoz, Moshe. *Palestinian Leadership on the West Bank: The Changing Role of the Arab Mayors under Jordan and Israel*. Totowa, N.J.: Cass, 1984.

Maoz is a knowledgeable and balanced Israeli academic expert on Arab politics and served for a time as adviser to the Israeli military governor of the West Bank. His book draws judiciously on both his academic and practical experiences.

Nyrop, Richard F., editor. *Jordan: A Country Study*. Washington, D.C.: Foreign Area Studies Division, The American University, 1980.

Plascov, Avi. *The Palestinian Refugees in Jordan 1948–1967*. London: Cass, 1981.

An exceptionally well-researched study of political activity among Palestinians on both the East and West Banks in the first ten years after Jordan took over the West Bank. Plascov has had access to interesting source material, expecially to Jordanian security services files captured by Israelis on the West Bank in 1967.

Smith, Pamela Ann. *Palestine and the Palestinians 1876–1983*. New York: St. Martin's Press, 1984.

An extensively researched account of Arab society in Palestine from 1876 (the year Abdul Hamid II acceded to the Ottoman Sultanate), expanded to include the Palestinians in Jordan and the diaspora after 1948. It is especially useful for its detailed, grass-roots picture of Palestinian life through the period.

Vatikiotis, P.J. *Politics and the Military Jordan: A Study of the Arab Legion, 1921–1957*. New York: Praeger, 1967.

Index

Irbid, 69, 76–77
Islam, 47–51; observance, 48–50; political-religious organizations, 48, 50–51; Shiite, 67; and society, 47, 66; Sunni, 67
Israel, 3; and Jordanian war with PLO militias, 77, 88; Labor-Likud coalition, 118; military forces, 83–84; military threat to Jordan, 85–86, 154; 1984 elections, 117–18; Occupation of West Bank, 31, 112–13, 124–25; Palestinian problem, 1, 4, 85; and West Bank, 111–15, 117–18, 131; as Western intrusion in Arab world, 47, 85; *see also* Arab-Israeli conflict; Peace settlement negotiations

Jerusalem, 9, 19, 23, 97, 98, 119, 131
Jordan, 141–43; arable land, 95; in biblical times, 9, 10; as buffer state, 3, 120; in classical period, 10–11; ethnic and religious minorities, 66–67; geography, 8–10, 82–83; human resources, export of, 98–99, 106–107; and changing Middle East, 3–4, 145; militarily indefensible, 82–83; as Occupied Enemy Territory (post-World War I), 14; under Ottoman rule, 11; Palestinian population, 21–22, 130–31, 141; and Palestinian question, 1, 2, 4, 61, 118, 141; and PLO, 32–33, 60–61, 75–78, 125–26, 135–37, 147–48; policy aims, domestic and foreign, 119; policy constraints, 119–22, 128–30; rapprochement with Syria, 137–38, 147–48; strategic role in Middle East, 90–92, 154; tribes, 14, 17
"Jordan for the Jordanians," 61
Jordan National Party, 43
Jordanian Peoples Government, 46
Jordanian Peoples Revolutionary Party, 46
Jordan River, 9, 83, 86
Jordan Valley, 8–9, 83, 97–98

Kahane, Rabbi Meir, 1
Kawasmeh, Fawd, 45
Khatib, Anwar, 124
Kirkbride, Alec, 14
Kissinger, Henry, 153
Kuwait, 97, 100

Labor force distribution, 104
Labor Party, Israeli, 117–18, 124, 146
Lebanon, 14, 84, 102, 110, 144, 153
Lewis, Bernard, 36

Likud bloc, 117–18, 124
Literacy rates, 68

Maan, 10, 11, 14, 16
Majali, Gen. Abdul Hadi, 92
Majali tribe, 14, 80
Mandates, League of Nations, 14
Mango family, 38
Manufacturing, 100, 102, 103 (table)
Mecca, 10,12, 13
Medina, 12
Meir, Golda, 20, 117
Mennonite Central Committee, 113
Middle class, 104–105
Middle East, 3–4, 144–45
Middle East Defense and Security Agency (MEDSA), 92
Ministries, Education, 48; Interior, 47, 52; Islamic Affairs and Holy Places, 48, 53; Supply, 108
Military, rule by, 35–36
Moabite Arab Government, 14
Mohammed, Prophet, 12
Monarchy, Hashemite, 27; and the army, 78, 81, 93; constitutional, 29, 55; Jordanian attitudes toward, 35–37, 142; 1957 coup attempt, 29–30, 36; and the social contract, 54–55; succession problem, 25–26, 54, 93, 142
Mukhabarat, 51
Muna, Princess, 3, 7, 25
Muslim Brotherhood, 38, 48, 64, 67, 85, 137

Nabateans, 10–11
Nabulsi, Suleiman, 29
Nadwa Palace, 7
Nashashibi family, 19
Nasser, Gamal Abdel, 28, 33
National Democratic Grouping, 46
National Democratic Party, 43
National Guard, 79
National Socialist Party, 29
Nayef, Emir, 7, 23
Noor, Queen, 3, 25
Nusseibeh family, 22

Obeidat, Ahmed, 38
Odeh, Adnan Abu, 133–134
Oil boom, 62, 98–101; effects of 101–105; levels off, 105–109; remittances, workers;, 98–99, 106–107, 115; subsidies to Jordan by oil states, 61, 99–100, 107, 116
Oman, 91
OPEC, 116

conference on Palestinian question, 146–47; military equipment supplier, 76, 82, 84–89; and PLO, 128
Students, 68–69; abroad, 3, 46–47, 52–53, 69 (table)
Subsidies, foreign, 61, 95, 99–100, 107, 111, 115, 116, 120, 155–56
Subversion, foreign-run, 45–46, 120
Suez crisis (1956), 29
Sunni Islam, 67
Syria, 3, 29, 32, 82, 98, 100, 120, 121, 135; attack on Jordan (1970), 76–77; destabilization of Jordan, 28, 30, 31, 45, 84–85; French mandate, 14–15; Golan Heights, 77, 84, 86, 147; and international conference on Palestinian question, 146–47; military forces, 83–84; as military threat to Jordan, 82, 83–84; rapprochement with Jordan, 137–38, 147–48; and United States, 147–48; uprising in Hama (Feb. 1982), 132
Syrian immigrants, 57–58, 97

Tabah family, 38
Tahrir Party, 48
Talal, King of Jordan (1951–52), 23
Tourism, 97, 102, 110
Transjordan, Emirate of, 14, 15, 16–18
Transjordan, Hashemite Kingdom of, 18
Tribes, 14, 17, 34, 70–71, 80
Tuqan family, 19, 22, 25, 57

Uneasy Lies the Head, 7, 23, 27, 28
Unemployment, 104, 106, 108, 116
Unionist Democratic Association, 42–43
United Arab Kingdom plan (1972), 123, 126, 131
United Nations, 18; Resolution for partition of Palestine (Nov. 1947), 19; Resolution 242, 122, 123, 136, 146, 149
United States, economic support for Jordan, 100, 120, 154–57; and Egypt, 2; interests in Jordan, 2–4, 28, 29, 145; and Israel, 148–51, 154; and Jordan's security, 152–54; and Jordan's strategic role in Middle East,

90–92, 154; Jordanian arms needs and negotiations, 89–90, 120, 152–53, 155; and Jordanian war with PLO militias, 77, 120, 153; and Middle East, 144–45; and peace settlement negotiations, 146–49; and PLO, 77, 149–51; recognition of Jordan, 18; and Syria, 147–48; subsidies to Jordan, 100, 155
University of Jordan, 68
UNRWA (United Nations Relief and Works Agency for Palestine Refugees in the Near East), 21, 27–28, 57
Urbanization, 68–70
Wahabis, 16
War with PLO militias (1970–71), 33, 60–61, 75–78, 98; fighting in Amman 75–76, 77; and Iraq, 76; Israeli alert, 77, 88; Syrian invasion, 76–77, 83; U.S. role, 77, 120, 153
West Bank, 4, 5, 97, 98, 139–40, 146–47; agriculture, 111, 112, 113; annexation by Jordan, 18, 20–21, 23; Camp David agreements, 99, 127; economic integration with Israel, 112–13; economy under Jordanian rule, 111–12; financial subsidies (Jordanian and other Arab states), 61–62; integration of infra-structure with Israel, 113, 115; Israeli occupation, 31, 112–13, 124; Israeli settlements, 124–25; Jordanian rule, 60, 111–12, 124; modus vivendi with Jordan and Israel, 118–19, 130–32, 143; money supply and banking system, 113–14; and negotiations with Israel, 125; and PLO, 124, 125–26; relations with Jordan, 113–15, 124–26; trade with Israel, 112–12; see also Peace settlement negotiations
West Bankers, 20–22, 101, 123; employment in Israel, 112, 115
Women, changing roles, 71–73

Yarmuk River, 82–83
Yarmouk University, 68

Zein, Queen Mother, 23, 24, 25–26
Zionism, 85

About the Author

ARTHUR DAY's acquaintance with the Arab-Israeli conflict spans his 28 years in the Department of State and the Foreign Service. In 1949–50 he served on what was then known as the Palestine Desk in the State Department, dealing with Israel and Jordan and the Palestinian question. After a series of other posts abroad and in Washington, he returned to Middle East affairs in 1967 with an assignment in the Department's Office of United Nations Political Affairs at the time UN Security Council Resolution 242 was being negotiated in the UN. A tour in the Arms Control and Disarmament Agency involved him in other matters from 1970 to 1972, when he was sent to Jerusalem as Consul General. In Jerusalem he was responsible for contact with affairs on the West Bank and Arab Jerusalem and visited Jordan from time to time.

Returning to Washington in 1975, he took charge of the State Department office responsible for Jordanian, Syrian, Iraqi and Lebanese affairs. A year later he was appointed a Deputy Assistant Secretary of State dealing, inter alia, with the Arab-Israeli conflict. During the first year of the Carter administration he focused entirely on American efforts to resolve the conflict. He accompanied Secretary of State Cyrus Vance to the Middle East in the summer of 1977 and participated in the negotiations in New York, in the fall of that year, with Israeli, Jordanian, Syrian and Egyptian delegations in an attempt to reconvene the Geneva Conference on Middle East peace.

He retired from the Foreign Service in late 1977 to become Vice President for Policy Studies of the United Nations Association of the USA. Since his retirement from UNA, Mr. Day has served as a consultant on foreign affairs.

166